SUPPORT
NOT SURVEILLANCE
How to solve the teacher retention crisis

DR MARY BOUSTED

First published 2022

by John Catt Educational Ltd,
15 Riduna Park, Station Road,
Melton, Woodbridge IP12 1QT

Tel: +44 (0) 1394 389850
Email: enquiries@johncatt.com
Website: www.johncatt.com

ISBN: 978 1 915261 16 8

Set and designed by John Catt Educational Limited

CONTENTS

INTRODUCTION

I begin this treatise – on behalf of and in support of teachers – with a simple premise. No education system can exceed the quality of its teachers. Teachers are the rock on which education standards are built. If there are not enough teachers in the right subjects and age phases to educate a nation's pupils then there are very real and very negative consequences for children and young people – consequences that are difficult to rectify in later life.

There have not been enough teachers in England for decades. School leaders report that their biggest professional problem is a shortage of teachers; successive governments have declared that this shortage is one of their top priorities. I have been in countless meetings in the Department for Education where this issue has been discussed anxiously and I have read many action plans to remedy the situation. None have worked because they fail to address the central problem: that teaching is not an attractive profession for graduates. When they can, graduates choose other professions, or they leave teaching in increasing numbers increasingly early in their careers.

It took a pandemic precipitating a collapse in graduate recruitment to allow the government to reach its secondary initial teacher training (ITT) targets for the first time in eight years. Yet, even with a 23% increase in new entrants to ITT in 2020-21 compared with 2019-20,[1] physics and maths recruitment did not reach target. More recent figures present a worrying picture of teacher training numbers returning to their pre-pandemic levels, with the latest data showing a 24% drop in applications.[2]

In Japan, 80% of teachers say teaching is their first-choice career. In Singapore, the figure is nearly 70%. England, by contrast, comes sixth from the bottom of the international league table, with just 60% of teachers saying the profession is their first choice.[3] Teaching should not be so low on the preferred list of graduate professions in England.

For those who do become teachers, motivated most often by a strong sense of public service and a desire to help children and young people, their experience may not fulfil their hopes and ambitions. Disappointed and disaffected, many leave the profession early to put their experience and skills to use in other professional roles. Teachers are attractive to employers. They are good communicators. They work collaboratively with others. They are problem-solvers. They are hard and conscientious workers. They are the most valuable asset lost to our education system. And once they leave the profession, often being very vocal about the reasons why, they overwhelmingly fail to return. And they do something else too: they tell others to avoid teaching.

The Covid-19 pandemic has changed the public's perception of teachers and the work they do. Parents who had to home-educate their children have learned that teaching is hard work; that getting children to learn is not always easy. They have seen their children's teachers revolutionising their work, with little or no training, in order to teach pupils remotely while also working in schools with vulnerable and key worker children. In January 2021, when the hapless Gavin Williamson admitted in a speech in the House of Commons that GCSE and A level exams would be cancelled for a second year, the then education secretary invited parents to contact Ofsted if they felt their children were not receiving high-quality remote education. It is telling that the inspectorate was overwhelmed with parents getting in touch to praise the work of teachers. The attempt to scapegoat teachers for the government's failings…failed.

LIFE-CHANGING TEACHERS

Celebrity testimonies to the work of teachers abound in the media. Four million people have watched a video of the former professional footballer Ian Wright bursting into tears in 2010 when, filming a programme at

Arsenal Football Club, he was reunited with his primary school teacher and mentor, Sydney Pidgen.

Hearing Mr Pidgen's greeting – 'Hello, Ian. Long time no see' – Wright looked amazed, snatching his hat off his head and later using it to cover his face as he cried. He had been told that Mr Pidgen was dead, but here he was, very much alive and 'so glad you've done so well for yourself' in the years since Wright left Turnham Primary School in south-east London.

Wright struggled at school. On *Desert Island Discs* in 2020, Wright remembered being outside the classroom when Mr Pidgen was walking down the corridor. He didn't look at him because he was terrified of the teacher who was 'so strict', whose suit was 'immaculate' and whose shoes were 'so shiny'. But Mr Pidgen looked at Wright and said, 'Come with me.' Wright says 'that changed my life'.

Wright told *Desert Island Discs*: 'I don't know why he chose me but he did. He gave me responsibility – I used to collect the registers from the teachers, then they made me milk monitor. It was really good, I just felt important. He wouldn't let me play football if he heard I'd been naughty in class. He just gave me a sense of feeling like I had some use … He was the greatest man in the world.'

During ITV's *An Audience With Adele*, broadcast in November 2021, the singer-songwriter Adele was invited by the actor Emma Thompson to name someone who had supported and inspired her in her youth. Adele answered: 'I had a teacher at Chestnut Grove [School in south-west London] who taught me English. That was Miss McDonald … she got me really into literature. I've always been obsessed with English and obviously now I write lyrics, but she also did street dance … In the canteen they used to do these dances and stuff like that … She was so bloody cool, so engaging. She really made us care and we knew that she cared about us … She was so relatable and likeable that I always looked forward to my English lessons.' Adele was then surprised on stage by Ms McDonald, whom she hadn't seen since she was 12. Tears were shed and Adele had to leave the stage to repair her makeup.

COMMUNITY CARETAKERS

'No one forgets a good teacher' is a truth backed up by many reminiscences in episodes of *Desert Island Discs* and newspaper columns on 'My best teacher'. This tells us something essential about teachers that government ministers over the past 30 years have forgotten in their quest to 'raise standards'. Teaching is, first and foremost, a human activity. Schools are mini societies where children and young people learn their rights and their responsibilities as citizens. School is where they experience life beyond their family.

In schools, with teachers as role models, pupils work with their peers – other pupils – who are the same age and live near them but who may be different from them in important ways. Learning to respect others, whether of a different race or culture, and learning to engage with and respect those who have different beliefs, is such an important life lesson for children and young people.

No one could deny the importance of children and young people learning the knowledge, skills and aptitudes they will need to prosper in life. But nor should anyone deny that schools teach values that enable children and young people to navigate a complex and fast-changing world. The family is the greatest and most important influence on children, but school is also very significant.

School is where children learn that they cannot just do what they like. It is where they make friendships that may last for life. It is where they experience triumph and disaster, often on a daily basis (what seems of little consequence to adults can often be felt very deeply by those who are experiencing something for the first time). School enriches their lives beyond measure.

Teachers do what they can to help the children in their care. They wash their school uniforms. They run food banks for families. They open on Christmas Day to serve lunch to children and their parents who can afford neither the turkey nor the electricity to cook it. They help parents fill in their benefit forms. They visit children's homes to make sure they are safe and well.

In a secondary school, teaching five lessons a day, teachers can encounter 150 pupils. They know all these pupils' names. They know something personal about nearly all of them. They look out for those pupils who are vulnerable; those who need safeguarding; those with special needs; those who are lonely; those for whom adolescence is difficult. Teachers are often the first to notice if a child is frightened or hungry, nervous or worried. They are usually the first to start the conversation that can lead to that child being helped. In the absence of a functioning Child and Adolescent Mental Health Service – where waiting times for young people who say they are suicidal can reach six months – teachers take on the burden of providing the support they can to these children.

Teachers are also responsible for the content and conduct of lessons, and how the subject matter is treated. They decide what activities the pupils will use to explore and understand the topic, and how they will gauge pupils' understanding. They consider the strategies they will use to support, extend and develop comprehension and pupils' ability to translate what they have learned into new situations.

Lessons are incredibly complex forms of human interaction. As well as learning about quadratic equations, the science of climate change or why Romeo says of Juliet 'O, she doth teach the torches to burn bright', children and young people are learning how to be part of the classroom community, where rules are necessary to enable others to learn. Pupils learn life skills that they can take with them into the world of work, where discipline is needed to arrive on time, do the job well and be part of a team. This discipline provides the basis for a life well lived, where others are treated with compassion and respect – even if you do not agree with them or like them.

EXHILARATED BUT EXHAUSTED

A teacher's day in school is full on and they are often exhausted when the school bell rings and pupils go home. In addition to teaching, which is very demanding, there will have been conversations with other teachers and with support staff. On some days there will be meetings, official and unofficial, and never-ending bureaucracy to be dealt with: data entry or reports on pupils who are 'cause for concern'.

According to a Trades Union Congress (TUC) survey, teachers work the most unpaid overtime of any occupation.[4] Primary teachers in England teach in classrooms for just over 24 hours a week; secondary teachers average 20.5 hours. But teachers in England top the Organisation for Economic Co-operation and Development (OECD) league table for working time outside lessons. In addition to their teaching timetable, primary teachers report spending nearly 32 hours and secondary teachers nearly 33 hours a week on non-teaching tasks such as lesson planning, marking, report writing and data entry.[5] There is clear evidence from the OECD that teachers in England find this burden more stressful than their international counterparts.[6]

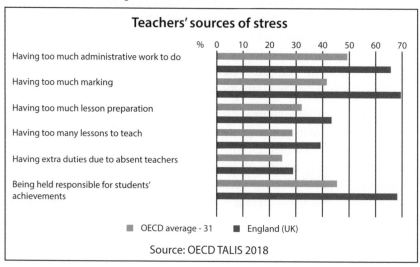

Teachers' sources of stress

OECD average - 31   England (UK)

Source: OECD TALIS 2018

Teachers have very little flexibility in their working day. They cannot decide to delay teaching a particular class, as those in other professions can decide to delay a difficult or boring task, until they feel more up to it. Teachers are on show in every lesson they take: maintaining a good learning environment; nipping 'trouble' in the bud; ascertaining who is engaged and who is not, and why this might be the case. Teachers have to cope with the unexpected, because children and young people do or say unexpected things. This level of constant alertness is often exhilarating – and exhausting.

Teachers work incredibly hard. As we will see in chapter 1, the stress of such intense and long working weeks takes its toll and results in appalling retention rates in the profession. Any sensible government really interested in raising educational standards would investigate what teachers do in their working weeks and ask the following questions:

- How much of this work is necessary to support effective teaching and learning?
- How much of this work does not support effective teaching and learning?

Any sensible government would then promote policies to strengthen the work necessary to effective teaching and learning and eliminate the work that is not.

No government, in my years as a teacher, a teacher educator and a union leader, has had the intelligence or the political courage to really address the long-standing issues that drive teachers out of the profession. No government has had sufficient will to keep teachers in the profession by tackling the causes of the unnecessary work that adds so much to teachers' working hours and to their stress levels. This failure has, more than anything else, depressed standards of education in England, particularly for the deprived children who most need well-qualified, experienced teachers in order to reduce the attainment gap between them and their more advantaged peers.[7]

This book is an unashamed, evidenced polemic. It gives an account of the state of the nation's teachers. The evidence base largely concerns teachers in England, because Scotland, Wales and Northern Ireland did not take part in the OECD's most recent (2018) Teaching and Learning International Survey (TALIS). However, I do not doubt that the pressures on teachers in those nations vary little from those faced in England.

In the end, there is one simple truth. Unless and until teachers achieve more rewarding working lives, the exodus from the profession will continue and so will the damage this inflicts on our children and young people. There is no more honourable profession than teaching. It is about time teaching was valued as such.

CHAPTER 1.
WHERE HAVE ALL THE TEACHERS GONE?

As we saw in the introduction, the failure to recruit enough trainee teachers is compounded by dire rates of teacher retention. Over the past three decades, successive education ministers and their civil servants have been acutely aware of the teacher supply problem and have attempted to reverse this worrying trend. None of these governmental and ministerial efforts have achieved positive results: teacher supply remains stubbornly insufficient.

The problem of teachers leaving the profession increasingly early in their careers has worsened in recent years, according to data from the School Workforce Census published annually by the Department for Education (DfE).[8] The 2020 census shows a decline in retention rates for each of the first five years in teaching. Of those entering the profession in 2011, more than a fifth left within three years; for the 2016 cohort, this rose to more than a quarter over the same period. The scale of the problem is revealed in the fact that in 2018-19, before the impact of the Covid-19 pandemic on retention rates, the number of teachers leaving for reasons other than retirement was around a third higher than in 2011-12.[9]

The problem intensifies as teachers spend more time in the profession. Within five years of qualification, 31.4% have left teaching. Within 10 years that rises to a whopping 40.8%.[10] You might have thought that older, more experienced teachers who had weathered the storm and could see retirement in their sights would lash themselves to the teaching mast and carry on in the classroom, but the leaving rates for teachers aged

50-59 remain high at nearly 13%.[11] These are not indications of a happy or healthy profession.

The reasons for teacher flight were investigated by the DfE in 2017.[12] Workload was identified as the top issue, followed by:

- Government initiatives/policy changes.
- Feeling undervalued by leadership/team.
- Ofsted pressure.
- Lack of support from school leadership.

All these issues will be explored in this book and, although they are identified as separate issues in the DfE survey, we will see that they are, in fact, highly interrelated. Teachers who identify excessive workload as a major problem blame the government for the frequent policy changes that add so much to their working hours as they rewrite their schemes of work and adapt to ever-changing national assessment requirements. School leaders' fear of Ofsted contributes to their unintended devaluing of teachers' knowledge and professional experience, which leaves teachers detached from decisions about curriculum, teaching and learning strategies and assessment. Workload is not only a matter of excessive working hours but also of high work intensity and low professional discretion.

HOW GOVERNMENTS HAVE RESPONDED TO TEACHER FLIGHT

The teacher supply crisis regularly erupts as a national scandal and places the government under pressure to act. One such eruption occurred in the late 1990s and early 2000s. Teacher supply, particularly in London, became a problem for the Labour government, which was persuaded to start talks that led to the National Agreement on Raising Standards and Tackling Workload in January 2003.

A multilateral Workforce Agreement Monitoring Group (WAMG) was formed as a social partnership with union, local and national government representation, in order to implement the agreement. The WAMG was to prove a positive and effective means for the government to ensure policy implementation in more than 20,000 points of service delivery. The group's achievements for teachers should not be underplayed: an end to a long list of admin tasks, much pupil supervision and most absence cover, with enhanced roles for support staff; a right to non-contact time for lesson preparation during the school day, which was a huge advance for teachers in primary schools; and a contractual right to work-life balance. However, this last provision, as subsequent chapters of this book will show, has not become a reality.

Even before any idea of partnership working was crushed by Michael Gove in 2010, and despite the best efforts of the WAMG, an uncomfortable truth remained: teachers' working hours were not reducing. The obvious reason was that governments were unwilling to move on their core school accountability policies. Ministers kept – and keep on – saying that they know excessive workload remains a problem and they will do anything to reduce it except the one thing that has the most impact.

In 2014, Nicky Morgan, Gove's successor as education secretary, issued a 'workload challenge'. Responses were submitted by 44,000 teachers, who told her that the biggest drivers of their excessive workload were 'in school' accountability tasks required by their leaders in readiness for Ofsted inspections. The DfE summarised the findings thus: 'The same themes were raised again and again by the profession as the key drivers of unnecessary and unproductive workload, including Ofsted and the pressure it places on school leaders (whether real or perceived), and from government – as well as hours spent recording data, marking and lesson-planning.'[13]

The government responded with a commitment to introduce minimum lead-in times for significant changes to accountability, curriculum or qualifications, and to conduct future surveys of workload. In 2016, three professionally led review groups advised that schools should collect only the minimum amount of data and shrink the volume of marking and planning. Two of the reports mentioned the demands of Ofsted. In 2018, the government published a Workload Reduction Toolkit and a report from the Teacher Workload Advisory Group.

All these exhortations to schools produced the following outcomes. In 2018, secondary teachers in England reported working an average 49.3 hours a week, against an OECD average of 41 hours and a 2013 figure of 48.2 hours. Primary teachers in England reported working 52.1 hours a week, more than in any other OECD participating country except Japan.[14] The DfE's 2019 workload survey found teachers working an average of 49.5 hours a week (4.9 hours less than reported in 2016), while senior leaders worked an average of 55.1 hours a week in 2019, compared with 60.5 in 2016.[15] Most teachers reported spending less time on lesson planning, marking and pupil supervision in 2019 than in 2016, but most still felt they spent too much time on these tasks.

These figures do not look good for the government. They tell us that teachers in England work longer hours than those in other countries, that much of the extra workload is a product of inspection and league table pressures, and that these perceived pressures trump any amount of advice and guidance from government. There are plenty of reasons why current school accountability is a mess, but its tendency to make teaching less attractive should be a stimulus to reform. Yet, to date, successive governments have resisted that reform because of a fear of appearing to be soft on 'standards'.

In 2017, the National Audit Office (NAO) published a coruscating report on the DfE's teacher supply strategy. It concluded that 'the Department has not set out in a coherent way and shared with schools and the teaching profession how they can work together to improve the teaching workforce'. The report also stated that the DfE's 'interventions to support the existing teaching workforce have been relatively small scale'.[16] The NAO said the DfE had 'limited evidence that its initiatives to retain and develop the teaching workforce are making a difference' and that teachers were 'increasingly leaving state-funded schools before they reach retirement'. Workload was described as 'a significant barrier to teacher retention'. Schools were 'finding it increasingly difficult to fill posts with the quality of teachers they need, which may have implications for the quality of education' – a factor compounded by the finding that teachers were 'undertaking relatively low levels of training and development, with schools reporting that time and cost are barriers to improving teacher quality'.

Stung by criticism that the DfE had no coherent strategy to recruit and retain teachers, Damian Hinds, then education secretary, issued a recruitment and retention strategy in 2019.[17] Announcing that 'there are no great schools without great teachers' and declaring that 'no other profession is as important in shaping the lives of the next generation', the document outlined four priorities:

1. Help create the right climate for headteachers and other school leaders to establish supportive school cultures – at the heart of which would be reform of the accountability system.
2. Transform support for early career teachers, in particular through the launch of the Early Career Framework (about which more later).
3. Develop specialist qualifications to support teachers who wish to stay and excel in the classroom, as well as those wishing to progress to leadership roles.
4. Radically simplify the process for becoming a teacher.

The strategy readily acknowledged that teacher workload in England was too high. It said:

'External pressures of accountability, change and challenging pupil behaviour can make leading schools difficult and demanding – particularly challenging schools. These factors can create pressure that is transmitted to teachers: headteachers can take actions that create workload and stress for teachers because they feel they have no choice, becoming more likely to over-control, over-track data and create defensive evidence to protect their school.'[18]

The strategy promised that a new inspection framework would 'rebalance inspection' towards the wider substance of what happens in a school'. Importantly, it would 'consider whether teacher workload is unnecessarily high as part of the [inspection framework's] Leadership and Management judgement' and 'look unfavourably on schools that implement burdensome data collection practices'.

Chapter 3 of this book will reveal just how ineffective the new (2019) framework has been in reducing teacher workload related to inspection. The sad fact of the matter is that education ministers have fiddled while teacher supply has burned. The consequences for teachers and their pupils of ministers' failure to act will be explored in the following chapters.

The tone of that exploration is urgent. I write with both sorrow and anger. The way we treat teachers in this country directly and negatively impacts on the way we treat children and young people. If we fail to establish adequate teacher supply then we compound the disadvantage already endured by the poorest children and young people – those who most need and are least likely to be taught by experienced, well-qualified teachers. The injustice of this should be obvious to all. Raising the status of teaching as a profession and ensuring adequate teacher supply would do much to narrow the achievement gap between poor children and their wealthier peers. It would be a concrete realisation of the current government's nebulous 'levelling up' agenda.

CHAPTER 2.
LOOKING FOR ANSWERS IN ALL THE WRONG PLACES

As the previous chapter has shown, teachers in England suffer from excessive workload that leads to an increasingly early exodus from the profession. Government efforts have not driven down teacher working hours.

On a Zoom call, 600 members of the National Education Union (NEU) were asked, in real time, to identify the causes of excessive workload in their schools and colleges. Their responses, through the magic of technology, were immediately transformed into the word cloud reproduced on the front cover of this book. The word cloud identifies accountability as the most significant driver of workload, in the form of marking, planning, data and – the enforcer of accountability – Ofsted.

If ministers were serious about reducing working hours, they would enact policies to help teachers focus on the core of their work. These policies would allow teachers to concentrate on what is important – teaching and learning in the classroom – rather than on creating a mountain of evidence that teaching and learning have taken place to an acceptable standard. The government knows from its own evidence, outlined in chapter 1, that accountability pressures and frequent education policy initiatives drive teachers to double their working hours, with time spent on lesson preparation, marking and administration exceeding the time spent actually teaching pupils.

An accountability overhaul and sustainable education reform would be the most effective ways for government to reduce workload, lessen stress and keep more teachers in the profession for longer. Reducing the administrative load is, according to international evidence, the single most effective thing that the government could do to mitigate the impact of the current teacher wellbeing crisis, because teacher stress is not heightened by the actual teaching they do in their classrooms but by the time spent on administration, marking and planning lessons.[19] (Just for the record: teachers accept that planning and marking are essential and important professional duties. Teachers resent the time they spend presenting their planning and marking in predetermined formats designed for accountability purposes rather than to inform their teaching and their pupils' learning.)

But, like the man who has lost his car keys in a muddy ditch, yet persists in searching for them under a street lamp on the opposite side of the road because the light is better there even though his keys are not, government ministers and civil servants continue to search anywhere and everywhere other than where they should look for the magic bullet that will stem the tide of teachers leaving the profession.

And so, initial teacher training has been the focus of considerable political interest recently. Nick Gibb, the former schools minister,[20] championed radical reform of the sector, convinced, despite all evidence to the contrary, that university education departments offering teacher training courses were stuffed to the gills with left-wing radicals whose main aim in life was to indoctrinate student teachers with their destructive ideology. This resulted in me, literally, banging my head against a DfE desk during a ministerial meeting as a way of relieving my frustration that there was no point in me, again, soberly and carefully laying out the evidence that Gibb's unshakeable belief was misplaced and misguided.

Gibb set in train a 'market review' of initial teacher training.[21] An 'expert advisory group' was established, its members notable for being either close to, or apologists for, Gibb's beliefs. The group's proposals were published to a storm of protest from the ITT sector. The Universities' Council for the Education of Teachers warned that the proposals could lead to a strict and inflexible curriculum for initial teacher training that would destroy the teacher supply base. Critics questioned why a review of ITT was necessary when all existing providers, at that time, were judged to be 'good' or 'outstanding'. ITT providers opposed the centralisation of the ITT curriculum and the prescribed approaches to assessment, pointing out that the requirements for mentoring student teachers in school would add considerable costs that were not recognised in the proposals. The University of Cambridge was among 35 ITT providers warning that they may be forced to end their involvement in teacher training.

And yet, despite the strength and depth of the opposition to the ITT reforms, as I write all ITT providers are in the process of applying for reaccreditation to ensure they have the capacity to meet the DfE's quality requirements for the training curriculum, placement schools, mentoring of trainee teachers and the framework by which students are assessed for recommendation of qualified teacher status.

As a model for education reform, the ITT market review follows a pattern that will be examined in more detail in chapter 5. It can be summarised thus: pack your 'advisory panel' with political allies and a token apologist who defends their collusion as 'working to improve things from the inside'. Portray those who disagree with your proposals as 'progressives' who carry the 'soft bigotry of low expectations' for poor pupils, and accuse them of working to undermine standards and rigour. Publish proposals that have had very little 'testing' in the sector and are, in significant part, practically unworkable. Release consultation documents packed with leading questions designed to support predetermined answers. Plough on through the ensuing controversy – the bigger the better because it entrenches your position, corrals your supporters and helps to wage the war on woke.

This tried-and-tested approach to reform doesn't always work. Ministerial power is never absolute. The implementation of the review was delayed for a year and significant amendments were made to its recommendations on training placements and mentoring. More scope was given to higher education institutions to define the research evidence on which their courses are based.

This is a marginally better outcome. But it is not the best outcome – and that was never going to be the case because the approach to policy reform was based on ideology rather than evidence, fuelled by ministerial zeal rather than rational analysis and driven by impossible timescales. If the 'expert advisory group' or Robin Walker, Gibb's successor as schools minister, had cared to look, there is clear evidence that teachers in England consider that their initial training prepares them well for teaching.

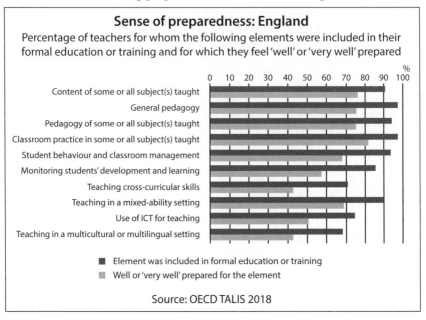

Sense of preparedness: England
Percentage of teachers for whom the following elements were included in their formal education or training and for which they feel 'well' or 'very well' prepared

Source: OECD TALIS 2018

According to the OECD's 2018 Teaching and Learning International Survey (TALIS), 86% of teachers in England were instructed on subject content, pedagogy and classroom practice – higher than the OECD average of 79%.[22] This theoretical training is complemented by a mandatory teaching practice in schools undertaken by 97% of teacher trainees, again significantly higher than the OECD average of 62%.

Where training is less successful is in using ICT for teaching – an essential professional competence during the Covid-19 pandemic, with the onset of remote teaching. Another area where trainee teachers feel less well prepared is in their monitoring of students' development and assessment of student learning. Assessment of pupils' knowledge and competence is key to teachers' future planning of the curriculum and to the teaching strategies they choose to adopt in order to help pupils overcome difficulties in comprehending and understanding the concepts they are being taught. But it is, for many reasons, particularly challenging for trainee teachers to use formative assessment to guide their teaching and their pupils' learning – they have not yet gained enough experience of their pupils' common misconceptions on key topics and, unsurprisingly, they have not had the time to develop a range of strategies for correcting pupil misunderstandings. Trainee teachers are also, in my 12 years' experience of working with them, very concerned about their ability to maintain good working relationships with their pupils. It is really daunting to take on the responsibility of teaching whole classes of pupils whose behaviour will, at times, be challenging and difficult. Trainee teachers need consistent support to learn how to create the best conditions for effective teaching and learning. The OECD evidence suggests that the majority of teachers report that they were well prepared for this core professional competence.

EARLY CAREER INDUCTION

Teachers, like all professionals, need the time and opportunity to develop their skills, deepen their knowledge and expand their abilities. Professional confidence, based on strong professional competence, is a great motivator – carrying teachers through the inevitable periods when they find their work challenging and difficult (and all teachers go through these times).

It should not be a surprise that a one-year teacher training course, whether higher education-led or school-based, cannot prepare beginning teachers for every challenge they will face in the early years of their teaching career, intensive though these courses undoubtedly are. Beginning teachers are on a journey to becoming more informed and more expert in their practice. Given the scale and nature of the demands placed on teachers – and given the fact that newly qualified teachers in England are more likely to be placed in schools where there are higher numbers of disadvantaged pupils and those for whom English is a second language – the fundamental importance of effective, high-quality, readily available continuing professional development (CPD) is obvious.[23] Early career teachers identify, in particular, the need for more support with: behaviour management; the use and understanding of assessment; specific pupil groups; subject and curriculum knowledge; pedagogical knowledge; lesson planning; and safeguarding.[24]

The government has recognised the 'career shock' felt by beginning teachers, introducing an Early Career Framework (ECF) supported by £130 million of extra investment every year to support its introduction and operation in schools.[25] Acknowledging that early career retention was a major issue, the support for beginning teachers of a 10% timetable reduction in their first year was extended, with a 5% reduction on their timetable in their second year.

The ECF is built around eight standards for beginning teachers and is intended to support them in: achieving high expectations of pupils' wellbeing, motivation and behaviour; understanding how pupils learn, including the importance of prior knowledge and working memory; developing a good knowledge of their subject(s) and curriculum; planning and teaching well-structured lessons; practising adaptive teaching by developing an understanding of different pupil needs; making accurate and productive use of assessment; managing behaviour effectively; and demonstrating the professional behaviours focused on wider professional responsibilities.

I think you can begin to see the problem here. Of course all these elements of teachers' knowledge, understanding and practice are important, but dividing them into eight categories – in order to build on the eight ITT standards – inevitably means that more time and effort must be taken to document progress in each section. And although the ECF guidance is clear (indeed, it is written in bold type) that '**the ECF is not, and should not be used, as an assessment framework**', early reports are that this is exactly how it is being used, with each section regarded as an assessment criterion on which the standards achieved by early career teachers are to be assessed. Using the term 'standards' in the ECF invites this response.

Early feedback indicates that the ECF, instead of being a support to beginning teachers, is turning out to be a burden – a three-year 'assessment' of their capabilities just at the time when the 'career shock' of new classes, new school routines, new discipline procedures, new schemes of work and teaching nearly a full timetable are being felt.

The response to the introduction of the ECF was overwhelmingly negative at a meeting of mentors for beginning teachers held in October 2021, two months after its country-wide implementation. Mentors and early career teachers reported that the workload involved in the framework was onerous; it was having a negative impact on the day-to-day support mentors felt they could offer to beginning teachers. The pre-reading for sessions and the requirements for 'self-study' in addition to the demands of teaching nearly a full timetable were, they told me, adding hugely to mentor and beginner teacher workload.

The mentors at the meeting – experienced teachers – felt the ECF was, in reality, having the opposite effect to supporting early career teachers. Mentors said they did not have the time in the school day to meet its demands and that the content was overly rigid and theoretical, failing to meet the concerns and needs of their new colleagues. Some ECF providers, they reported, were holding sessions at the end of the working day or on Saturday mornings, without consideration for beginner teacher workload or equalities issues. Most concerning of all, they told me that their headteachers were saying they would not employ a newly qualified teacher in the future – an example of unintended outcomes if ever there was one!

A poll conducted by the National Association of Head Teachers in 2021 revealed that a third of the school leaders who responded feared the ECF, designed to support new teachers, would drive people out of the profession because of the level of workload the framework is creating for early career teachers and their mentors. The vast majority (95%) of heads agreed with the proposition that the ECF had increased workload for newly qualified teachers, with 64% saying the ECF will have a negative impact on the work-life balance of early career teachers. Equally worrying is the finding that 99% of heads said the ECF has had an overwhelmingly negative impact on the work of mentors.[26]

It is early days, but the ECF is in danger of realising all the problems of centralised government educational initiatives. Led by a determination to do different and do better, too many are undone by excessive ambition. A desire to be game-changing – in this case, to radically improve the retention rates of beginner teachers – has resulted in an overstuffed, highly theoretical ECF curriculum that is built on eight (too many) standards and has become an assessment, not a support framework.

The ECF falls foul of another systemic problem in our schools: there are not enough mid-career teachers to support their beginner colleagues.

Remember that 40% of teachers leave within 10 years, just at the time when they would be able to offer their experience and knowledge to more inexperienced colleagues. Those teachers who do stay will almost certainly be overloaded with curriculum and pastoral responsibilities over and above their full teaching timetables. If they work in primary schools they are very likely to not be paid for those responsibilities. So, becoming a mentor in addition to a full teaching timetable and additional professional responsibilities is a very big ask – one that many mid-career teachers regretfully decline because they have insufficient time to do it well.

The ECF is a good idea, but it is overly ambitious in its content, overly technical in its application and under-resourced in its implementation, without the infrastructure – in this case, enough experienced teachers with enough time in their working day – to make it work.

This problem is not confined to the early stages of teachers' careers, however, as the next section of this chapter will show.

CONTINUING PROFESSIONAL DEVELOPMENT

One question I always ask when I meet teachers is whether they are getting access to the CPD they need. Generally, I get a negative response. Teachers tell me that CPD is rationed because of strained school budgets, and too often refused because leaders are concerned about pupil progress if their regular teacher is absent. So, if teachers are going to engage in CPD then it is in their own time. The problem is, of course, that teachers' excessive working hours constrain the time they have available and are willing to invest in their professional development. It is hard to do more when you are already exhausted.

Secondary teachers in England are increasingly concerned about the cost associated with their CPD activities. Whereas 44% agreed or strongly agreed in the OECD's 2013 TALIS that expense was a barrier to their CPD activities, this increased to 56% in 2018. The 2018 figure was above the OECD average (45%), with expense, followed by conflicts with work schedules (65%), identified as the key reasons why secondary teachers in England reported not completing more CPD.[27]

The lack of time and investment in CPD is a real cost to the profession and to the pupils it serves, because the effects of high-quality CPD throughout teachers' careers are significant, particularly for pupil learning outcomes. High-quality CPD can close the gap between beginner and more experienced teachers, adding a remarkable 10 years to beginner teacher competence, and has a greater effect on pupil attainment than other interventions schools may consider, such as implementing performance-related pay for teachers or lengthening the school day.[28]

CPD is often understood primarily as attendance at externally provided training. Teachers value this provision because it gives them the opportunity to meet colleagues away from the pressures of the busy school day in order to invest in their own professional learning. But teachers also value school-based professional development, working together to share experience and expertise – for example, through peer observation or collaborative work on curriculum development. This is more likely to be effective in developing professional practice because it is rooted in the shared context of the school's pupil intake and the shared context in which teachers work.[29] Building on the foundations of teachers' initial professional education and recognising different stages of development throughout teachers' careers, effective school-based CPD enables teachers to reflect on their practice, grow in professional confidence and skills, and develop particular aspects of their role.

School leaders play a key role in promoting professional growth among teachers, and in whether or not teachers are supported to develop their skills. Research shows that leaders who demonstrate their respect for their colleagues through support for their professional learning are more able to retain their staff.[30] There are particular characteristics of schools where leaders have created the conditions for teachers' professional growth and development to thrive. These elements of the professional environment include:

- Peer collaboration among teachers, who work together to refine their teaching practices and to solve problems.
- Sufficient time and resources for professional development.
- A school culture characterised by mutual trust, respect, openness and commitment to student achievement.

- Teacher evaluation that provides meaningful feedback, helps teachers to improve their instruction and is conducted in an objective and consistent way.[31]

So, to what extent does the English school system display the characteristics that enable teachers to grow professionally through peer collaboration? Do teachers feel trusted and respected? Is the evaluation of their work meaningful to them and does it help them to improve their classroom practice?

THE WORKING LIVES OF TEACHERS IN ENGLAND

The hugely influential OECD Directorate of Education and Skills, led by Andreas Schleicher, conducts TALIS to compare key facets of teaching and learning in OECD countries. There have been three TALIS surveys: in 2008, 2013 and the biggest yet in 2018, which had 48 participating countries including China (Shanghai), Japan, the US, Singapore, South Africa, New Zealand, the UAE, Norway, Chile, the Czech Republic and Russia.

The two-volume, 450-page report on the 2018 TALIS explores in great detail the ways and extent to which educational systems internationally support teacher autonomy and professional expertise.[32] Volume II is subtitled 'Teachers and School Leaders as Valued Professionals', which makes its results particularly pertinent to the considerations of this book; it provides the evidence base for much of this chapter.

The most important conclusion to be taken from TALIS is that the way teachers are treated in England is abnormal by international standards. England is an outlier in its treatment of teachers – and not in a good way. Other high-performing nations treat their teachers better and take positive action to develop their potential and protect them from excessive work. These nations understand the maxim that no education system can exceed the quality of its teachers. They pursue policies to make teaching attractive to graduates and encourage them to remain in the profession.

Using survey evidence gathered from teachers and leaders in the participating countries, the report on TALIS 2018 makes 52 recommendations (perhaps diplomatically termed 'policy pointers') to governments about the most effective ways to support teachers and leaders and to improve their national education systems. The report also provides international comparative evidence on how effectively, or otherwise, individual participating countries are creating the conditions for teacher and leader professionalism.

The problem is not that English teachers lack appraisal of their work. England comes second in the OECD international league tables, behind Singapore, in terms of the volume of feedback received by teachers.[33] The methods of feedback measured include: lesson observations (with England at the top of the 'lesson observation' league table[34]); the external results of students (e.g. national test scores); and self-assessment of the teacher's work (conducted in the English system largely through appraisal and performance-related pay).

So, how effective is all this feedback in making a positive impact on teacher's practice? Unfortunately, as is so often the case, quantity does not mean quality. England comes at the lower end of the OECD league table for teachers who report that the feedback they receive has a positive impact on their practice.[35]

I have lost count of the number of times teachers have told me that they feel overly monitored by managers who fail to ask them any questions about their knowledge (of the pupils) or their expertise (in teaching). One memorable conversation was with a teacher who had just finished an MA course in the teaching of reading; she was regularly being given 'cut down' commentaries on research on the latest methods of teaching reading, based on the work of academics who had taught her on the MA course. She had never, not once, been asked for her informed opinion on the teaching of reading in her school.

Of course, a responsibility for whether, and what, pupils have learned is an important element of teachers' professional duty. In the past, teachers whose performance was inadequate too often faced insufficient challenges and consequences. I am not arguing that our schools should return to the 1970s, where the progress and achievements of Black pupils and working-class pupils were held back because of low expectations and inadequate professional monitoring by leaders of their teachers' work.

What I am arguing is that teachers would feel more positive about their responsibility for pupils' outcomes if they had more say in how those outcomes were achieved – and in particular more say in decisions about teaching, learning and assessment strategies. Yet teachers in England do not expect to be asked for their opinion on decisions that affect them – a worrying fact evidenced by the finding that England comes third from the bottom of the OECD league table, far below the OECD average, on whether schools allow for teachers to actively participate in school decisions.[36]

Teachers' perceptions that their opinions are not sought or valued are corroborated by school leaders, who report that they spend less time supporting their teachers, collaborating with them to develop teaching and learning approaches, and much more time (towards the top of the OECD league table) ensuring that 'teachers feel responsible for their students' learning outcomes'. The difference between the time spent by school leaders in England monitoring their teachers and the time they devote to working cooperatively with teachers to develop new teaching practices is stark.[37]

The silencing of teachers' voices on professional issues has profoundly negative consequences for the English education system. According to the OECD, teachers who feel respected for their professionalism, through careful attention being paid to their professional views, are more likely to engage their pupils in learning activities that are interesting, challenging and transform pupils' previous understanding.[38] These teachers feel more able to engage their pupils in what the OECD calls 'cognitive activation strategies', which demand pupils' attention and require their active engagement in learning, resulting in the transformation of knowledge for the pupils' own ends. This is real rather than rote learning. These teachers report higher levels of job satisfaction, which is such an important part of the decision they make – at two, five and 10 years into their teaching careers – to stay in or to leave the profession.

Teacher self-efficacy – their belief that they have expertise and are confident to use their knowledge and skills in their teaching – is essential to making this an attractive and rewarding profession. As Schleicher notes:

'The concepts of teacher self-efficacy and job satisfaction are ... important to schools and education systems ... it is not just about making sure that teachers are happy and feel good about their roles and their teaching, although, of course that is important as well ... there are positive associations between both self-efficacy and job satisfaction and student

achievement. High levels of teacher self-efficacy are also associated with student motivation and other positive teacher behaviours. Conversely low levels of self-efficacy can be linked to greater stress and problems with students who misbehave. Job satisfaction is important in itself as it relates to teachers' level of commitment to the profession, and, in turn, schools' ability to retain the best teachers.[39]

Surely it is not too much to expect that teachers should be given responsibility and agency over wider aspects of school life and school decision-making? Distributed leadership in schools would mean teachers being given a professional voice in helping to determine: school assessment policies (given their close relationship with the curriculum and with course content); school disciplinary policies (given that teachers implement and enforce those policies); equal opportunities policies (given that teachers' understanding and confidence around these issues are essential if these policies are to be more than just statements filed in a cabinet in the school office). And so on.

In many OECD countries, teacher representatives have a role on the school senior management team, so the voice of the classroom practitioner and their experience can inform collective decision-making. Meanwhile, England comes 40th out of 48 in the OECD league table for teacher involvement in the school management team.[40]

The OECD's TALIS evidence tells us one important truth: the working conditions of teachers in England are poor by international standards. It tells us that other high-performing nations treat their teachers much better than we do; that in these countries teachers lead more fulfilled professional lives in which their expertise is valued through their involvement in important decisions in their school. It tells us that teachers in other high-performing nations are monitored less intensively, allowing professional confidence and growth. It tells us that teachers' work, confidence and commitment could be better valued and better utilised in England.

If there is one finding from TALIS that should alert us to the parlous state of teacher wellbeing in England it is this: 38% of teachers in England, more than double the OECD average, report that they experience a lot of stress in their work. England comes a shameful second in the OECD league table of teacher stress, a finding that should be met by the government, and by employers, with an urgent, serious response.[41] Instead, the government has decided to withdraw from future TALIS surveys. Perhaps the international comparisons are just too stark?

Another important research study has revealed another important truth: that within Britain the quality of teachers' working lives has deteriorated when compared with all other professions, while the intensity of their work has risen to unprecedented levels. The British Skills and Employment Survey (SES) collects data from working adults in England, Wales and Scotland roughly every five years.[42] Participants are interviewed in their own homes, with one eligible adult per address randomly selected for interview. Although the SES is designed for all workers, schoolteachers are covered in sufficient numbers to illuminate trends in teachers' job quality.

Two indicators of job quality are assessed in the SES: 'work intensity', which is defined as the rate of physical and/or mental input to work tasks performed during the working day; and 'skills and discretion', which includes the influence teachers have over decisions about the tasks they do, how those tasks are performed, how hard they work and the quality standards to which they work.

The results of the SES are alarming. There is no other word for them. Since 2012, teachers' work intensity has soared. By 2017, 90% strongly agreed that their job requires them to work very hard – a remarkable finding and particularly so considering that just 52% of other professional occupations reported the same level of work intensity. The researchers conclude: '**No other large occupation has shown anything like this degree of work intensification.**'[43]

The intensification of teachers' work has been accompanied by a similarly alarming decline in the discretion that teachers are permitted to exercise over their work. The SES reveals a dramatic decline in the extent to which teachers report that they can participate in decision-making in their schools. In 1992, 45% of teachers reported that they had either 'quite a lot' or a 'great deal' of say over organisational changes; in 2017 this proportion had reduced to just 20%.

Work intensification and low task discretion combine to produce high work strain. Teachers are nearly twice as likely as other professionals to be working under high strain. In 2017, 85% of teachers reported that they came home from work exhausted, with only 45% of other professionals reporting the same. Not surprisingly, the SES reports that teachers' contentment score is substantively below other professions. (It is also interesting to note that teachers in Scotland report much lower work intensity than elsewhere in Britain, so we do not have to look far afield, geographically, to see that the profession could be treated much better in England.)

Another important finding from the SES is that teachers' belief in their job security – the one advantage teachers felt they had over other professions – is now gone. Other professions have caught up in the job security stakes. Teaching, according to those who teach, appears to have few attractions.

Taken together, the TALIS and SES surveys tell a damning tale. Teachers in England are reporting high levels of distress about their lack of professional agency, revealed in very low discretion over what they do and how they work. Is it surprising, then, that the retention rates for teachers are so poor? And what damage does poor retention do to the education of the nation's children and young people?

It is notable, also, that the deterioration in teachers' conditions of work occurred most starkly in the past decade, at the time when government ministers were most insistent that their policies were leading to freedom and autonomy for the profession. These important international and national surveys tell a different story – and the reverse of what the government has claimed.

Both TALIS and the SES reveal a sad loss of a collaborative culture in English schools, replaced by a culture of compliance and control that robs teachers of their standing and experience as professional educators. The absence of a collaborative culture in schools infantilises teachers, diminishing their agency and denying them professional choice and discretion.

A huge waste of talent, commitment and expertise results from the hierarchical conditions in which too many teachers in England work. How much better could working and learning be in our schools if teachers were given the respect they deserve for their professionalism, and if leaders were supported in their efforts to create a cooperative and collaborative ethos in their schools? How much more effective would government policies to reduce excessive and intensive teacher workload be if they were focused on eradicating the causes of these evils, rather than treating them as an inconvenient truth, ignoring them and hoping they will magically go away? (They won't.)

I do not believe that it is the intention of England's school leaders to run compliant rather than collaborative schools where teacher voice is muted and professional experience and expertise are wasted. There is much talk now, and some government action, on teacher wellbeing. There is also talk of distributed leadership. But in the absence of clear and regular feedback channels, it is too easy for leaders to believe their own narrative: that teachers in their schools are involved in key decisions and policy development, when the opposite is far nearer to the truth.

If we accept, as I do, that school leaders would prefer to lead schools with a collaborative, professionally respectful ethos rather than command and control, then the question must be: how have we ended up with a pervasive culture, in too many schools, that results in the silencing of teachers' voices; that results in repression and compliance rather than cooperation in the shared pursuit of the best education possible for pupils? This question is the subject of the next chapter.

CHAPTER 3.
OFSTED'S CULTURE OF COMPLIANCE

'The management of mistrust in an education system can be very expensive'
– Andreas Schleicher[44]

In the same month that Ofsted was created in 1992, the then Conservative government released its general election manifesto, pledging to 'introduce, for the first time, regular independent inspection' to give information to parents on the performance of all local schools, 'enabling them to exercise choice more effectively' and providing them with 'straightforward reports on their child's school, together with an action plan from governors to remedy any weaknesses'. This was part of a wider drive within the election manifesto to 'extend competition and accountability in public services'.

The sense that public services were failing and that strong measures needed to be taken to remedy the situation was reinforced when Chris Woodhead, Her Majesty's Chief Inspector from 1994 to 2000, said he wanted Ofsted to be a 'weapon of fear and terror' to teachers. It was also Woodhead who said, with no justification or evidence, that 15,000 teachers were 'hopeless incompetents'.

Thirty years on from these inauspicious beginnings, Ofsted is championed by government ministers as the guardian of educational standards in schools and colleges, providing indispensable information for parents. The many damaging outcomes of inspection (attrition in the teacher workforce; the naming and shaming of those schools, disproportionately with disadvantaged pupil intakes, that receive negative Ofsted grades and thus find it much harder to recruit and retain teachers and leaders) are justified by Ofsted as the necessary consequence of 'telling it as it is' and not letting the context in which schools operate become an excuse for poor educational standards.

Ofsted's reputation as a reliable judge of school standards is remarkable. Various DfE officials have told me, when I raise serious issues about the agency's operation and impact, that they understand and to a greater or lesser extent (depending on the issue) share my concerns. But they believe there is very little they can do. Ofsted is, it seems, politically impregnable. I have been told that the DfE is loath to challenge Ofsted because it will not get government backing. This has been true of Conservative, Labour and coalition governments.

Ofsted reports make media headlines. Current and past chief inspectors are wheeled out for frequent media interviews on education stories, and Ofsted's recommendations carry great weight in government policymaking. Ministers may be irritated when Ofsted is critical of their policies, but the appointment of chief inspectors who are, shall we say, closely aligned to government thinking helps to keep their relationship on an even keel.

All this happens despite the fact that Ofsted is a regulatory agency despised by the profession it regulates. When asked what should happen to Ofsted, 86% of NEU teacher and leader members said it should be abolished; 41% of those members wanted the agency to be abolished and not replaced, and 45% said they wanted it abolished and replaced by another inspectorate. Only 4% of respondents wanted Ofsted to stay as it is.[45]

All professions are wary of their regulator, but teachers hate and leaders fear Ofsted – with good reason. One poor inspection result too many is career-ending for leaders and career-shaming for teachers. The shadow of the inspectorate looms over the profession, driving practices that teachers say are workload-intensive but useless. Leaders admit they would not engage in the intensive monitoring practices outlined in the previous chapter – practices that add hugely to the excessive workload and stress felt by teachers and contribute greatly to the creation of compliant rather than collaborative education workplaces – were it not that they constantly have a weather eye, and sometimes an intense gaze, on what they believe the inspectors will want to see when their school gets the call.

This anxiety about having the right evidence when the inspector calls is heightened by Ofsted's apparent inability to decide what evidence it requires. Ofsted has changed its inspection framework five times in the past nine years as it struggles to find a method that does more than confirm the pupil intake of a school. The more deprived the pupil intake, the more negative the Ofsted judgement – a troubling finding that will be explored in more detail in the next chapter.

Despite Ofsted's protestations that it does not require any special preparation for its inspection visits, the truth is that even a small change in the inspection framework generates huge amounts of additional work, as school leaders, and then teachers, readjust, rewrite, revise and repurpose their teaching aims, curriculum, behaviour policies, attendance policies, leadership and management policies, and so on.

Bigger revisions to the inspection framework – such as in 2019, when Ofsted made a startling U-turn away from examining school data and towards a focus on curriculum – cause a tsunami of work, as leaders and teachers move heaven and earth to provide the new evidence that they think, they have heard, they imagine, Ofsted will demand to see. Ofsted has admitted that its previous inspection frameworks supported the enforcement of negative educational practices – in itself an admission that its judgements are invalid because they have measured the wrong things. In a startling admission for an agency that might have 'never apologise, never explain' as a strapline, the chief inspector, Amanda Spielman, said:

'For our part, it is clear that as an inspectorate we have not placed enough emphasis on the curriculum. For a long time, our inspections have looked hardest at outcomes, placing too much weight on test and exam results when we consider the overall effectiveness of schools. This has increased the pressure on school leaders, teachers and pupils alike to deliver test scores above all else.'[46]

Driven by a new zeal, out went the old and in came the new. Out went 'in-school data' – inspectors would not, at any price, cast their eyes over the 'evidence' they had previously pored over. In came curriculum plans –

with a focus on curriculum content, progression and pupils' understanding of key concepts. Ofsted confidently asserted that its latest inspection framework would be fairer to schools working with disadvantaged pupil intakes because the link between pupil data and inspection judgements had been severed. That ambitious claim will be examined in the next chapter.

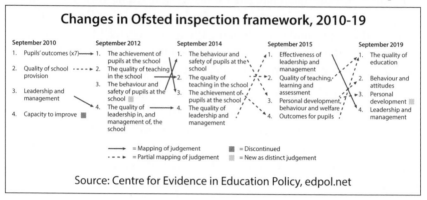

Changes in Ofsted inspection framework, 2010-19

Source: Centre for Evidence in Education Policy, edpol.net

NEU membership polling clearly demonstrates the extent to which Ofsted dominates the workload of leaders and teachers. In focus groups, teachers and leaders told us of the monitoring activities they utilised or were subject to in schools. This information was used to create workload categories for wider polling of the membership, who were asked what evidence they were required to submit to senior managers and/or the monitoring activities they were required to engage in. Of the teachers surveyed, 73% were expected to provide reports on pupil progress, 52% had to supply evidence of lesson planning and preparation, 77% underwent lesson observations and 71% were required to give feedback to pupils in pre-defined formats. These findings strongly endorse those of TALIS 2018, explored in the previous chapter.

The ways in which teachers' work is monitored are various and onerous. Some – like providing feedback in a particular style, including marking in different colours – have proved to have no merit in giving effective feedback to pupils. Lesson observations are a very poor way of ascertaining the quality of a teacher's work in the classroom and/or the quality of pupil learning, because even with experienced observers who are following explicit criteria, there can be enormous variations in their judgements of a lesson.[47]

The extent to which the latest Ofsted inspection framework dictates in-school monitoring of teachers and generates workload is revealed in the finding that 77% of the teachers surveyed by the NEU report that they are required to submit evidence in the form of book scrutiny, and 66% to provide evidence of 'curriculum sequencing'. Neither category would have been recognised or required before the 2019 inspection framework. The emergence of curriculum sequencing and book scrutiny as monitoring practices in schools are evidence that the most recent changes to the framework do not, as Ofsted claims, reduce teacher workload. They merely create new forms of bureaucracy for teachers.

When asked whether they felt these monitoring practices were a good use of their professional time, teachers' answers were hugely negative: 80% felt that having their lesson planning monitored was not helpful, 79% were of that opinion when it came to providing feedback in a particular style, and 73% felt book scrutiny was unhelpful. Learning walks and lesson observations fared slightly better: only 65% of teachers felt these practices were unhelpful, which is a positive way of framing what is still a big negative. Teachers felt strongly that they should not have to undergo many of these monitoring requirements. In particular, more than 70% objected to providing feedback in a required style, which correlates with the TALIS 2018 finding that teachers in England spend considerably more time marking than their international counterparts.

As the prospect of an imminent inspection looms, the internal monitoring activity in schools increases and intensifies. In the NEU polling, 56% of teachers and leaders reported that more than 50% of their working time was consumed by Ofsted preparation in the run-up to an inspection. That is a remarkable statistic borne out by anecdotal but frequently repeated tales told to me of teachers and leaders, when the notice period before an inspection was longer, spending the whole weekend in school before the inspection commenced on the Monday. The current inspection practice of one day's notice has not, it would appear, relieved the pressure of a notice period; rather it has encouraged a permanent state of 'battle-readiness' for when the inspector calls, which could be tomorrow.

The extent to which Ofsted dominates teachers' working lives, even when there is no imminent prospect of an inspection, is revealed by teachers' own words in an NEU survey. Let their voices be heard here:

'We have an LA advisor who has told us we need curriculum progression maps on the website for Ofsted, so I have a day's cover this week to write their curriculum plan for RE. I've literally been shown how to cut and paste it from some other school's document, but with some changes to "make it look like ours". All the forms have to look the same, apparently, to be corporate. I got to pick the colour of the heading for the form. Red was taken so I got pink. It's a joke – but it's not funny.'

'I work from 7.30am to 6pm every day and on weekends too – often 10 or more hours. I work most holidays including Christmas … All I perceive is more demands and much of the workload is about demonstrating things to others, e.g. Ofsted, the local authority, subject leaders, and putting work on walls and making classrooms look a certain way rather than being aimed at teaching children.'

'I have moved from the state sector (academy MAT) to the private sector this year … The difference is astounding. I felt totally unable to use my professional judgement in my previous workplace due to Ofsted accountability (even during Covid), but I now I feel like I have more autonomy. I feel disappointed that I have been "forced out" of the state sector, but I was left with no choice as I needed to protect my mental health.'

'The expectation to be Ofsted-ready while juggling the day-to-day teaching and my mental wellbeing make work a constant worry that just keeps building.'

'The senior leadership team are under immense pressure from the prospect of Ofsted dropping in at any moment. People are scared and frightened. SLT say, "We're not doing this because of Ofsted." But they are. People are frightened and it affects everyone in the school.'

'Ofsted just seems to release more and more things for us to do. Ofsted needs to change. I'm not saying there should be no accountability but to not have the same box-ticking exercises.'

IS IT ALL WORTH IT?

If the evidence was clear that Ofsted was a force for raising standards of education then the workload, stress and pressure caused by its inspections might be justified. So, how effective is Ofsted in raising school standards? How reliable are its judgements? That is to say, if two inspection teams visited the same school, how comparable would be their inspection judgements?

And here's another question: how *valid* are Ofsted inspections? That is to say, do inspection judgements measure the quality of a school's education provision, or do they measure something else altogether?

The short answer to these fundamental questions is: we simply do not know. And neither does Ofsted. Because, as Tom Richmond of the think tank EDSK notes, 'Since it was created over 25 years ago, Ofsted has not published any research to support the notion that their judgements on schools accurately reflect the quality of education that a school provides.'[48] Strangely, and some would say shockingly, the inspectorate has no evidence to support its assertion that the grades it awards are an accurate reflection of the quality of the education being delivered in a school, because it has no evidence of the extent to which its inspection practices measure education quality.

Because learning is something that happens internally, within pupils' heads, Ofsted relies on proxies for learning: lesson observations and more recently work scrutiny. Yet it has no evidence that these inspection practices, and the inspection judgements arising from them, reflect teaching quality and pupil learning.

Presumably, Ofsted regards every one of its frequently changing inspection frameworks as valid, and perhaps that is why it has done no research into what would appear to be a fundamental area of enquiry. What this means is that Ofsted's strapline, 'raising standards, improving lives', can only be described as an aspiration because it has no evidence, other than the judgements it awards schools, that it is raising school standards. Ofsted's claims in this regard, based on the percentages of schools awarded 'outstanding' or 'good' grades, are entirely self-referential. There is no evidence that the increasing percentage of schools being awarded 'good' Ofsted grades correlates with an actual rise in educational standards. Although this might indeed be the case, it is equally possible that it is not. That was the conclusion reached by the NAO in its 2018 report on Ofsted, which includes this statement: 'Ofsted does not know whether its school inspections are having the intended impact: to raise the standards of education and improve the quality of children's and young people's lives.'[49]

As discussed earlier in this chapter, the 2019 inspection framework claims to move away from tests and exam results, and towards inspection that judges the extent to which the 'intent, implementation and impact' of a school's curriculum result in a deep and rich learning experience for pupils. The framework is predicated on the belief that Ofsted inspectors – who do an average of nine days' inspection each year, because most of them have full-time jobs as school leaders – can, over a two-day inspection, come to valid and reliable judgements on the quality of a school's curriculum through 'deep dives'. These so-called deep dives are intensive immersions into a subject area, or an age phase, involving lesson observations, work scrutiny and interviews with the teachers responsible for leading the subject or phase. These generalist inspectors will, in the main, have no degree in nor experience of teaching the subject or the age in which they are conducting the deep dive.

Before the introduction of its latest inspection framework, Ofsted conducted small-scale studies into the reliability of its inspection judgements, testing the extent to which different inspection teams, faced with the same evidence of education provision in a school, would come to the same judgement about its quality and award similar inspection grades. Her Majesty's Inspectors (HMIs), the most experienced tier of inspectors employed in that role full-time by Ofsted, were asked to scrutinise work on four indicators, one of which was pupil progress. Ofsted claimed that the reliability of the inspectors' results was good – a claim that was quickly countered when it was revealed that none of the four indicators produced reliability scores above 0.5 and one indicator produced a score of just 0.38 (a score of 1 would indicate complete agreement between inspectors).[50]

Even more concerning is the finding that these numbers were an amalgamation of primary and secondary schools. When secondary school inspection was considered separately, there was greater disparity between inspectors' judgements. Inspectors involved in the research study reported that they found it difficult to come to judgements about the quality of the curriculum in subjects in which they were not qualified. As EDSK's Tom Richmond has written:

> 'Remember that the inspector who visits your school could well be a non-specialist in the subject they are inspecting. To cap it all off, Ofsted admitted that work scrutiny might not be possible in special schools, it may not work in further education and skills, it probably won't be any use when judging "alternative methodologies in teaching and learning" (e.g. Montessori schools) and it might not produce anything useful for modern foreign languages.'[51]

It is hard to see why these disappointing findings on the very poor reliability of inspector judgements on curriculum quality could not have been foreseen. As one critical commentator noted ahead of the introduction of the 2019 inspection framework, 'How will inspectors be equipped with the detailed knowledge and skills to make valid and reliable judgements on the extent to which the curriculum of a subject they have not taught, nor studied at degree level, is well planned and well sequenced? How are inspectors going to assess whether the curriculum reflects the school's local context when they will spend, on average, two days in that locality?'[52]

Every public service and the profession that works within it must accept proper and thorough accountability, in the absence of which very bad things can happen. Without proper accountability, poor professional practice can go unchecked and discrimination against particular service users can go undetected and unaddressed. As public servants, teachers and leaders must be accountable for the work they do.

But teachers and leaders should have confidence that their work will be expertly judged; that inspection grades will be reliable and not dependent on the inspection team that arrives at their school gate. They deserve the reassurance that their professional reputations will not rest on shaky foundations: on inspectors' knowledge and understanding (or lack thereof) of subjects and age/phases in which it is entirely possible that they have no teaching experience and poor subject knowledge.

In the absence of these routine requirements, teachers and leaders suffer under the yoke of Ofsted. Actually, too many teachers and leaders cast off this yoke and leave the profession, because of Ofsted. The 44,000 teachers who responded to Nicky Morgan's Workload Challenge in 2014 identified in-school accountability practices – data collection (56%), marking (53%) and planning and preparation (38%) – as the biggest drivers of their excessive workload. The burden of these tasks was increased by accountability measures and the perceived pressures of Ofsted (53%) and by the tasks set by managers (51%).[53]

Eight years later, as the evidence in this chapter has shown, the form of in-school monitoring practices has changed in some respects, but the damaging effects on teachers' working lives remain and are testimony to the constant pressure to provide 'evidence' to meet the requirements of the current Ofsted framework. Teachers are exhausted by the length of their working week and by the intensity of their work, so much of which they find unproductive. Ofsted is a major factor in all these negatives.

Any government serious about raising standards of education would seriously consider fundamental reform of an inspection system that has lost the confidence of the profession whose work it judges. Ofsted needs either substantial reform in order to render its judgements valid and reliable, or abolition so that a new form of inspection can be established.

And there are signs, now, that Ofsted is facing a credibility crisis. It is not just the usual suspects who are critical of the way it works, the fear it engenders in the profession and the dubious quality of its judgements. A recent YouGov poll carried out for the University of Exeter found that two-thirds of parents don't consider Ofsted reports when choosing their child's school and that nearly three-quarters pay no attention to performance tables that rank schools according to exam and test results.[54] Remarkably, this is true even of middle-class parents, a minority of whom refer to Ofsted reports when choosing their child's school.

Alison Peacock, chief executive of the Chartered College of Teaching, launched a wholly unexpected broadside at Ofsted when giving evidence to the Times Education Commission in 2021. She told the commissioners: 'Teachers are constantly looking over their shoulder, whether it's about

Ofsted judgements, whether it's about attainment, whether it's about workload ... Ofsted, frankly, it's a reign of terror.[55]

At times the self will intrude, so let me confess here that I am a survivor of more than 25 Ofsted inspections. Working in education departments in three universities, and as head of education in one, I toiled under a punishing inspection regime. I gained extensive experience of inspections of primary and secondary initial teacher training in a wide range of subjects and age phases. An imminent inspection certainly piled on work for me and my colleagues – so much so that a whole room was routinely dedicated to house the paperwork demanded by inspectors. Hours were spent preparing files on every aspect of teaching and learning, curriculum and assessment, all cross-referenced against the teacher training standards. Tables were arranged around the room, piled high with multiple files containing lecture notes, student assignments and course documents.

Although I am happy to acknowledge that over the course of my 12-year university career I met some excellent inspectors, with very good subject knowledge and forensic faculties that shone light on weaknesses in course provision or assessment, I also suffered too many inspectors who had woeful gaps in their subject knowledge, and inspectors whose judgements were so poor that, after months of intensive effort plotting a path through Ofsted's labyrinthine appeals process, they were overturned.

All of which points to one deduction. Based on my own exhaustive professional experience, I am certain that Ofsted has major problems with quality control, and that those problems go right up to the level of HMI. Ofsted inspectors' knowledge, experience and expertise are uneven. Too often – and this must increasingly be the case with the 2019 inspection framework, which is focused on the curriculum – inspection teams' expertise is inadequate for the subject or age range that they are called to inspect.

Ofsted is despised by teachers and discredited in their eyes. The shadow it casts over schools drives teachers and leaders to find other work in which they can gain greater autonomy and agency. The fact that no government in the past 20 years has been prepared to delve into this serious issue – to think seriously about how it might be addressed and then act upon it – shows a fundamental lack of seriousness of purpose when it comes to raising standards of education. It also reveals cowardice, where fear of tackling a difficult issue (namely, radical reform of inspection) trumps the drive to ensure there are enough teachers in the profession to educate the nation's children.

Ofsted is in dire need of radical reform. A modest proposal of how that reform might be achieved is put forward in chapter 6.

CHAPTER 4.
THE CRUSHING IMPACT OF CHILD POVERTY

I often wonder why teachers are held responsible for the poverty of their pupils. It is readily accepted that the lineaments of poverty – dilapidated and overcrowded housing, poor diet, increased stress and poor mental health – are major factors in the decreased healthy life expectancy of the disadvantaged. But when teachers and leaders cite poverty as a critical and major factor in the attainment gap between poor children and their better-off peers, they are accused, by politicians and others, of imposing the poverty of low expectations on those pupils. Why do health professionals get support and praise for working in deprived communities, while teachers and leaders are blamed and shamed for doing the hardest work among the poorest in our nation?

Education staff working in schools that serve deprived, left-behind communities encounter every day the damage that poverty inflicts on children and young people. Teaching in any school is a very demanding job, but teaching in schools for the poor – and there *are* schools for the poor, because our schools are highly stratified in terms of their social intake – places further pressures and demands on staff.

These demands are growing, because the numbers of children living in poverty are growing. The causes of poverty are many, intergenerational and complex, but recent government policy has made matters much worse. Between 2010 and 2016, the Conservative/Liberal Democrat coalition government and then the Conservative government implemented policies with an economic impact that included more than 40 cutbacks and changes to benefits and tax credits. Couples with children were left, on average, £2,080 a year worse off, with lone-parent families £1,940 poorer.[56]

Unsurprisingly, given these cuts to family income, the number of UK children living in poverty in working households soared by 800,000 between 2010 and 2019. The rate of child poverty in working families rose to 2.9 million in 2018 – an increase of 38%. In 2010, according to analysis by the TUC, one in five children in working households (19%) were growing up in poverty; by 2018, this had increased to one in four (24%).[57] By 2019, in an average class of 30 pupils, nine were living in families officially classed as poor.[58] But it was not just families with children who were losing income.

I found it astonishing that Chancellor Rishi Sunak, in his budget statement in the House of Commons on 28 October 2021, boasted that he was restoring school funding to 2010 levels, in real terms, by 2024, hoping to garner praise for a government that had presided over no real-terms growth for 15 years. His chutzpah was noticed by Paul Johnson, director of the influential Institute for Fiscal Studies (IFS), who noted that the UK education budget will have risen by just 3% by 2025 against 2010 levels, compared with a 40% increase on health spending. Commenting on this 'remarkable lack of priority', Johnson said: 'You would expect it [education funding] to rise at least in line with the size of the economy, if not faster, and it hasn't. This is not a set of priorities which looks consistent with a long-term growth strategy.'[59] And despite Sunak committing himself to the 'most wide-ranging skills agenda our country has seen in decades', the extra £3.8 billion allocated for skills training will leave funding for FE colleges 10% below and sixth-form college per-pupil spending 23% below a decade ago.[60]

Pre-16 school funding fared a little better than post-16 funding between 2009-10 and 2019-20. According to the IFS, spending per pupil in England fell by 9% in real terms, the largest cut in over 40 years.[61] But schools in deprived areas inexplicably faced the largest falls in funding, with secondary schools in the areas with the 20% lowest incomes seeing their per-pupil spending cut by more than £1,000 – from £8,169 in 2009-10 to £6,996 in 2019-20.[62]

Secondary school spending per pupil by quintile of eligibility for free school meals (2021-22 prices)						
	Q1 (least deprived)	Q2	Q3	Q4	Q5 (most deprived)	All schools
2009–10	£6,249	£6,232	£6,491	£6,968	£8,169	£6,772
Change	–£568	–£480	–£463	–£530	–£1,173	–£602
Real-terms growth	–9%	–8%	–7%	–8%	–14%	–9%
2019–20	£5,680	£5,753	£6,028	£6,439	£6,996	£6,170

Source: Institute for Fiscal Studies

Schools have had increasing numbers of children with greater needs at a time when their funding has been cut by the largest amount in over 40 years. Even more inexplicably, the national funding formula has continued this pattern by providing bigger real-terms increases for the least deprived schools (8-9%) than for the most deprived ones (5%) between 2017-18 and 2022-23.[63] So much for levelling up.

It is not hard, I think, to understand how damaging has been the combination of a huge rise in child poverty and cuts of nearly a tenth in school funding. The effects of child poverty are recorded in the NEU's annual survey of the education state of the nation. In 2019, NEU members' reports of the extent of child poverty in their schools were particularly shocking. Nearly half felt that, to a large extent, child poverty was a significant factor hampering their pupils' learning and a further 33% agreed that this was the case 'to some extent'. One member commented:

'The poverty gap has clearly got bigger. The number of students displaying difficult behaviours has increased and poverty is most certainly a factor.'

A significant number of members described concern about school uniforms:

'Several wear clothing that is ill-fitting or not clean. Shoes are often ill-fitting or very worn, coats are often inadequate for weather.'

'We have bought uniform items and pretend they are from students who have grown out of them.'

'Children coming to school with holes in their shoes or cheap shoes which are not weatherproof. Children attending school with no coats, no socks and without other essential items of clothing.'

'Dress-up days can be ... a very sad day. The rich children show off and those struggling with finances are really noticed by the other children ... so they may decide not to attend school on that day.'

'Food banks are an everyday necessity, as is the market for either free or second-hand uniform. Parents have no spare money and children are suffering.'

When asked in a multiple-choice question to identify the impacts on learning that could be attributed to poverty, over three-quarters of respondents noted that their pupils demonstrated fatigue (78%), poor concentration (76%) and poor behaviour (75%). More than half said their students had experienced hunger (57%) or ill health (50%) as a result of poverty, and more than a third (35%) said students had been bullied because of it.

NEU members told us of 'overcrowding in homes, so children do not have space to do homework', and that 'far more students are finding it hard to concentrate'. One wrote: 'Most of my class arrive at school hungry and thirsty.' Another: 'Some students have mentioned that they have not had any food for two days; some come without having breakfast and with no dinner money but are not on free school meals.'

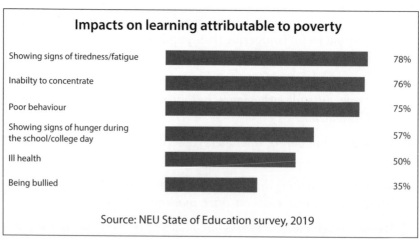

Impacts on learning attributable to poverty

Showing signs of tiredness/fatigue	78%
Inabilty to concentrate	76%
Poor behaviour	75%
Showing signs of hunger during the school/college day	57%
Ill health	50%
Being bullied	35%

Source: NEU State of Education survey, 2019

It is hard for those who have never witnessed child poverty so acutely to understand just what a toll it takes on children and young people. But child poverty also takes an awful toll on education staff. One of the main motivations for entering teaching is to help children and young people and to prepare them for their future lives. But when those futures are damaged and denied through poverty then education staff carry that burden with them – throughout the school day and into their home lives. They are upset by what they witness and exhausted by the scale of the deprivation they encounter.

It should be obvious to everyone that children who are hungry or cold, tired or anxious will find it more difficult to learn in school. Obvious to everyone apart from, apparently, the politicians and commentators who support the austerity policies despite their impact on poor families. And so it is that teachers, school leaders and union leaders who cite endemic and systemic levels of child poverty as a major cause of educational underachievement are accused of being apologists for poor teaching and low expectations, which supporters of austerity claim are the causes of the lower educational outcomes achieved by deprived children and young people.

But this is not true. One startling fact gives the lie to the charge that it is teachers' low expectations that are responsible for the poorer educational attainment of deprived children. **The fact is that 40% of the educational attainment gap between advantaged and disadvantaged children emerges before they start school.**[64] The damage done to poor children begins even before their birth. It is astonishing that thousands of babies in England are still being born prematurely, smaller than their expected birthweight or stillborn because of socioeconomic and racial inequalities. Research involving more than one million births suggests that poverty accounts for a quarter of stillbirths, a fifth of preterm births and a third of cases of foetal growth restriction (FGR). One in 10 stillbirths and almost one in five FGR cases are due to racial inequalities.[65]

These facts alone should make it obvious that teachers cannot, however hard they try (and their efforts are unremitting), inoculate deprived children and young people against the damage that poverty inflicts upon their lives and prospects. To hold teachers, uniquely of all professions, responsible for the effects of poverty on children's development is fundamentally unfair. It is unjust. And it makes working in schools for the poor a fraught and uncertain choice. It is a choice made even more difficult by the fact that schools in deprived areas, serving poor children with the greatest needs, have faced the most savage government spending cuts. It is shameful that the poorest secondary schools received a 14% real-terms cut to per-pupil spending between 2009-10 and 2019-20, compared with a 9% drop for the least deprived schools.[66]

This inequality is compounded by the equally savage cuts to funding for local authority support services for disadvantaged children and young people. Central government support for local authorities (LAs) in England nearly halved between 2010-11 and 2017-18[67] – cuts that were a consequence of central government distrust of local democracy, which left LAs with little choice but to lay waste to their support services for disadvantaged children and their families. The Sutton Trust has estimated that there were 1,000 fewer children's centres in 2017 compared with 2009,[68] and local funding for youth services fell by 40% between 2010 and 2017.[69] These cuts have fallen hardest on the children and young people who most need the services. A survey by the National Youth Agency found that children in affluent areas of England were twice as likely to have access to youth clubs and other out-of-school activities as those in poorer areas, and that youth buildings were more than twice as likely to be purpose-built for or dedicated to young people in affluent areas than in deprived ones.[70]

Such swingeing cuts to LA support services put teachers and leaders even more in the eye of the storm. They are left to cope without the support services they previously relied on. One by one they see the demise of speech and language therapy, family liaison officers, special needs advisers and so on. One statistic indicates the scale of the unmet need: the number of pupils referred to Child and Adolescent Mental Health Services by schools increased by a third between 2014 and 2018. However, around 31% of those referred and in need were declined the help they needed.[71]

The scale of this unmet need has a profoundly negative effect on teachers, support staff and leaders working in disadvantaged schools. Their working lives, already stressful enough, are made much worse as they struggle – against a backdrop of declining budgets in their schools and severely declining levels of support services in their local authorities – to support children and young people experiencing severe challenges in their lives and the greatest need for compensating support.

A rational response to the increased challenges faced by the profession because of government policies would be to offer more support: better funding for schools generally and particularly for those in deprived areas; stronger support services around schools; recognition and praise for the work that education staff are doing in such adverse circumstances. But we do not live in a rational world. We live in a world of toxic, shocking and profoundly unjust blame and shame. As I write, today, an anonymous Tory MP is quoted in a national newspaper: 'No one has properly taken to task shit teaching, shit schools and shit headmasters.'[72] (Let it be understood that this Tory MP, under the cloak of anonymity, is only saying what many MPs on the right, and some on the left, think.) The coarseness of this expression betrays the MP's contempt for teachers and leaders.

DOES OFSTED FAIRLY JUDGE THE QUALITY OF EDUCATION IN SCHOOLS IN POOR AREAS?

There is a widely held belief that schools in disadvantaged areas provide a poorer education than those in the leafy suburbs. Ofsted plays a central role in furthering this belief because it disseminates, through its inspection judgements, misinformation about the work of teachers and leaders in these schools and the standard of education they provide.

NEU analysis of Ofsted data[73] reveals that the more deprived a school's intake, the more it is likely to receive a negative Ofsted grade. The correlation between pupil poverty and a negative Ofsted judgement is particularly strong in secondary schools: secondaries with the fewest poor pupils are three and a half times more likely to be judged 'outstanding' than those with the highest intakes of poor children, which are nearly six times more likely to be judged 'requires improvement'. Further NEU analysis reveals that, since 2005, 666 schools have only ever been judged 'requires improvement' or 'poor' by Ofsted. Of those, 53% have intakes in the most deprived quintile, 28% have intakes in the second most deprived quintile and just 1.5% have the least deprived intakes.

Phase	Free school meals band	Ofsted Outstanding	Ofsted Good	Ofsted Requires Improvement	Ofsted Serious Weaknesses	Ofsted Special Measures
Primary	1. Highest	7%	64%	13%	0%	1%
Primary	2. High	8%	67%	10%	0%	0%
Primary	3. Average	9%	68%	8%	0%	0%
Primary	4. Low	15%	65%	5%	0%	0%
Primary	5. Least	23%	57%	3%	0%	0%

Phase	Free school meals band	Ofsted Outstanding	Ofsted Good	Ofsted Requires Improvement	Ofsted Serious Weaknesses	Ofsted Special Measures
Secondary	1. Highest	8%	45%	23%	2%	3%
Secondary	2. High	9%	56%	16%	1%	1%
Secondary	3. Average	9%	61%	14%	1%	1%
Secondary	4. Low	17%	61%	8%	1%	0%
Secondary	5. Least	29%	39%	4%	0%	1%

Source: National Education Union

This data shows that teachers and leaders' belief that Ofsted judgements are unfairly stacked against them is valid; that their concern that their professional reputation and future employability might be harmed by choosing to do the hardest work with the most deprived pupils is not without foundation. Given Ofsted's apparent bias against serving in schools in deprived communities, it is easy to understand why those schools find it so much harder to recruit and retain qualified and experienced staff. Most negatively, the Ofsted hurdle means that the pupils in those schools, who most need experienced teachers qualified in the subjects they are teaching, are less likely to get them.

Faced with these criticisms, Ofsted frantically revised its inspection framework five times in nine years. As described in chapter 3, this culminated in a framework heralded as a significant move away from a focus on pupil data and towards inspection of the quality of a school's curriculum. Ofsted claimed this would result in fairer judgements on schools with deprived pupil intakes, because the grades would be based on the quality of the curriculum rather than pupils' attainment.

However, the promise of fairer Ofsted judgements on schools with deprived pupil intakes has not been realised. These schools continue to disproportionately receive negative grades.

Of course, Ofsted is not going to admit – and indeed it strenuously denies – that its inspection judgements are based on the relative advantage or disadvantage of schools' pupil intakes. While conceding that disadvantaged schools generally have a harder job to do, Amanda Spielman, the chief inspector, argues that parents want the 'absolute comparison' with schools serving different and more advantaged pupil intakes and that taking into account the characteristics of a school's pupil intake would promote lower expectations for pupils in poor areas of the country. Ofsted must, Spielman asserts, continue to be an honest broker that reports without reference to the levels of poverty among a school's pupils.[74]

This might, of course, be an argument that holds water. Some parents might want absolute judgements of education quality, unaffected by qualitative measures such as the level of education readiness of a school's pupils on intake, or the progress made by these pupils during their time in the school. However, the YouGov survey described in chapter 3 indicates that those parents are in a minority: the majority of parents make no reference to Ofsted reports on their child's school.[75] This decision may be influenced by their realisation that the reports are out of date, partly because of an exemption for 'outstanding' schools that is no longer in force, and partly because Ofsted is inadequately resourced to inspect schools according to its timetable.[76]

But the problem for Ofsted, and even more so for teachers and leaders working in disadvantaged schools, is that its inspection judgements do not even provide this 'absolute comparison'. Groundbreaking research by the Education Policy Institute, which should have attracted much more attention when it was published, raises fundamental questions about Ofsted's inspection judgements.[77] It reveals that, using a robust measure of school performance based on value-added measures over three years (to safeguard against one-year blips in performance), schools in deprived areas with challenging pupil intakes that made significant *gains* in performance were disproportionately likely to be judged as 'requires improvement' or placed in special measures. Conversely, schools in the leafy suburbs with advantaged pupil intakes that over a three-year period made similar *declines* in value-added performance were likely to be judged by Ofsted as 'good' or 'outstanding'. Most damningly of all, the researchers concluded that Ofsted was better at judging the characteristics of a school's pupil intake than the quality of the education it provides.

Ofsted judgements are a huge factor in making it more difficult for the most disadvantaged children and young people to be taught by the experienced, well-qualified teachers they need. Schools serving disadvantaged communities experience greater recruitment difficulties, particularly in the secondary sector. Teachers in the most disadvantaged secondary schools are twice as likely to report that their departments are not well staffed with suitably qualified teachers, compared with schools with the most affluent intakes. These shortages are worst in the core subjects of maths and sciences, where one in three departments in schools serving the most disadvantaged communities say they are currently not well staffed.[78]

It is not hard to fathom why deprived schools find it so much more difficult to recruit and retain teachers and leaders. In addition to the increased challenge of working in these schools, facing and dealing with the horrors that child poverty inflicts upon pupils' lives and futures, teachers and leaders live and work under the constant threat that their efforts will be misjudged by Ofsted, their school shamed by an unfair inspection judgement and their careers damaged or ended. For many school leaders, an inadequate Ofsted judgement is the end to their career.

It should be obvious that teachers and leaders should not be blamed for the much poorer educational outcomes caused by child poverty in this country. It should be recognised that children who suffer deprivation and distress in their early lives – because they are poor, because they have an inadequate diet, because they live in overcrowded accommodation with nowhere quiet to learn, because they are cold, because they witness distress among parents and carers and family dysfunction – will begin school with significant and lasting harm to their ability to learn. The effects of this harm will intensify as they grow older, leading to a widening of the education gap between them and their more advantaged peers.

Our education system compounds its deliberate neglect of poor children through the practices of Ofsted, an inspection agency that gives inaccurate and invalid inspection judgements that shame leaders and teachers working in schools with high levels of pupil deprivation. These professionals, who are doing fantastic work in the most difficult of circumstances, are left with the responsibility but without the resources to change the lives of poor children.

HAVE WE ACHIEVED BETTER SOCIAL MOBILITY?

In the aftermath of searing criticism of the government's 'unforgivable'[79] failure to make contingency plans for the replacement of GCSE and A level exams in the Covid-hit years of 2020 and 2021, a lively and public debate was stimulated on the use of timed exams as the dominant mode of assessment in the award of levels at GCSE and grades at A level. Four commissions launched by *The Times* newspaper, the Edge Foundation, Pearson and the NEU ran concurrently to investigate the secondary school curriculum and its assessment, with some also considering the nature of the teaching profession. The formation of so many commissions is an indication that fundamental questions are being asked about the current arrangements for the curriculum and its assessment.

Speaking at the Social Market Foundation in 2013, Michael Gove, then education secretary, defended the hotly contested revisions to the national curriculum that were then going through the process of publication in draft form. It is a long speech, clearly written by Gove himself, in which he sets out the case for 'powerful' knowledge as a moral force giving poor children the same cultural and intellectual inheritance of their more advantaged peers in public schools.[80]

Drawing heavily on the work of ED Hirsch Jr, the American educational thinker and writer, Gove argued that the aim of education should be to inculcate the acquisition of knowledge that had, hitherto, been the preserve of the elite. In so doing, children from poor backgrounds, with parents who lacked the means to purchase a private education, would be given the intellectual capital on which to build their economic and social capital. Bemoaning the fact that ex-public school pupils dominated the cabinet and shadow cabinet, newspaper editorial teams, the FTSE 100 boardrooms, the nation's galleries and bishop's palaces, Gove accused the progressive educational establishment of entrenching inequality because of its focus, over the past 40 years, on following the child's interests, rather than delivering a knowledge-rich curriculum that he characterised as a 'set hierarchy of knowledge – literary canons, mathematical proofs, scientific laws, musical exercises and artistic traditions'. The tone was urgent as Gove asserted that 'unless that knowledge is imparted in school then students from poorer homes will continue to perform less well in the exercise of every basic skill that one needs to be employed in the modern world'. (Note the implied connection here between powerful knowledge and skills. The link between them is not explored but it is asserted.)

It is not the purpose of this book to explore further whether Gove's characterisation of the supposed ills of progressive education practice have any basis in fact – others have done that. For the record, I profoundly disagree with this characterisation. Let us, rather, consider Gove's key rationale for powerful knowledge – that it would equip poor children with the knowledge and skills to succeed economically and to gain access to the top professions. My question is: has that laudable aim been achieved?

The latest data from the Education Policy Institute[81] shows that the attainment gap between disadvantaged pupils and their peers has stopped closing. By the end of secondary school, a disadvantaged pupil is on average 18.1 months behind their peers in overall attainment for maths and English – the same gap as five years ago. The gap at primary school increased for the first time since 2007, which may signal that the gap is set to widen in the future. This was the situation even before the Covid-19 pandemic.

The researchers note that the worsening of the attainment gap has coincided with a growing proportion of children living in persistent poverty, but also that the gap has worsened since 2017 for three of the other five disadvantaged groups (including the least persistent two). They write:

'It is not just a compositional shift towards higher persistence or poorer outcomes for this group that explain the worsening trend in the gap. Factors affecting disadvantaged pupils as a whole – including the rise in poverty depth over the two decades and the squeeze on per pupil school funding and other public services since 2010 – are likely to have contributed.'[82]

NEU analysis of GCSE results awarded nationally, sorted by quintiles of pupil deprivation, show that in 2016 secondary pupils in schools teaching the least deprived young people were 68% more likely to achieve expected grades than pupils in schools teaching the most deprived students. In 2019, following reforms to GCSEs, that figure had risen to 106%.[83]

It is, of course, difficult to disentangle the root causes of these disappointing findings. But one thing is clear: powerful knowledge has not transformed the educational achievement of poor pupils, nor their life chances. There could be several reasons why this is the case.

An inclusive curriculum, as defined by UNESCO's International Bureau of Education, 'takes into consideration and caters for the diverse needs, previous experiences, interests and personal characteristics of all learners. It attempts to ensure that all students are part of the shared learning experiences of the classroom and that equal opportunities are provided regardless of learner differences.'[84]

Our current school curriculum does not meet this definition. It does not meet the diverse needs of different learners and has depressed the achievements of the most disadvantaged. The sharp distinction made by advocates of powerful knowledge between that powerful knowledge and everyday knowledge further and disproportionately disadvantages working-class pupils and those from some ethnic minorities. These pupils see fewer examples in the taught curriculum drawn from their culture, fewer role models from their communities and fewer aspects of their everyday lives reflected in the school curriculum.

The Black Lives Matter movement has raised awareness of the 'colonising' of the curriculum and the under-representation of Black artists, writers, thinkers and scientists in the school curriculum.[85] Parallel questions can be asked, of course, of women and working-class writers and artists, scientists and mathematicians.

The question of who decides what is 'powerful' is not new. Writing in the 1950s, the cultural historian Raymond Williams argued that in the process of producing and reproducing a cultural heritage, there is a selection and reselection by the dominant group in society 'of those significant received and recovered elements of the past which represent not a necessary, but a desired continuity'.[86] These choices are not, Williams argues, neutral: those literary and artistic works included in the canon speak to the values and interests of the powerful. What is excised from the cultural canon is the work of those who are not members of the powerful elite and whose interests in and representation of the world do not align with – and indeed challenge – the elite.

The disproportionately large gap between disadvantaged pupils' lived experience and the school curriculum may be one explanation of the failure of powerful knowledge to close the achievement gap. There may be another reason for this failure. Could it be that the powerful knowledge in the national curriculum is, in reality, not anything like powerful enough?

One outcome of the two long periods of remote learning necessitated by the Covid-19 pandemic was the experience of many parents of home-schooling their children. If education was, as in Jim Callaghan's famous 1976 speech, a 'secret garden', it is no longer. Some of those parents are very well informed: Dr Kit Yates, for example, a senior lecturer in the department of mathematical sciences at the University of Bath, told *The Guardian* he was shocked by how many different and 'intimidating' methods and models primary pupils were expected to use to solve basic maths problems. He concluded: 'I've never needed to use them – you don't need to know all these different mental models to do maths.'[87]

Erin Kelley, a bestselling novelist who teaches creative writing, called the English curriculum being taught to her seven-year-old daughter 'practically Dickensian'. She told *The Guardian*: 'It's not about the content of what they're saying, or its effectiveness. It's about labelling every word in a sentence until the idea of language itself is just horrible to children.'

And there was a bit of a rebellion by Lucy Kellaway, the well-known late entrant to teaching who, after a successful career as an associate editor at the *Financial Times*, wrote in that paper about the return to school on 8 March 2021:

> *'When I go back to school next week, I will have no choice but to buckle down and teach GCSE economics exactly as the OCR exam board tells me to. I will obediently tell pupils that there are advantages and disadvantages to countries of rising productivity – and that one of the*

disadvantages is that if one country increases its productivity then others might follow suit and end up overtaking it.

'It pains me to teach such bilge. I despise the limited way of thinking that says you need two advantages and two disadvantages to everything and you must structure every six-mark answer in the same way. It is boring, stupid and bears no relation to the economy.'[88]

All this begs a bigger question about the current national curriculum. The OECD data that will be explored in chapter 5 notes that England is in pole position for the use of rote memorisation as a teaching and learning tool, as reported by teachers and their pupils.

When asked why this was the case, Andreas Schleicher, director for education and skills at the OECD, replied: 'The English education system is disproportionately dominated by exams. Your children face more exams than nearly any other country. Exams focus on the reproduction of subject knowledge content, so why would teachers invest in cognitive elaboration strategies?'[89]

The 'cognitive elaboration strategies' that Schleicher is referring to are learning activities that promote enquiry, investigation, consideration of evidence, teamwork and communication. He is clear that not enough of these strategies underpin teaching and learning in English schools, and that this lack is leaving young people unprepared for the real world, where collaborating on problem-based learning activities that require interdisciplinary content knowledge is on the rise.

Another uncomfortable truth is that the route march through content is intensified by the presentation of knowledge that is required by the exams that so dominate children and young people's education prospects. So much rests on these exams that the complexity of the subject matter, as Kellaway asserts, is compromised by the required format of the exam answer – to the point where the 'knowledge' students download on to the exam paper, in timed and stressful conditions, is so reduced and simplified as to be plain wrong. It is not knowledge necessary to unravelling the complexities of the matter. Nor is it an essential training for the future lives of young people as professionals, parents and people – citizens of an increasingly complex, interdependent world.

The result, according to Yates, is that a 'significant amount' of his work in teaching first-year undergraduates involves 'undoing the half-truths' students have been fed in school. 'Maths can be a really creative subject. I wish there were time built in to just explore,' he says.[90]

And then there is the question of skills development, because the challenge to Gove's comfortable elision between powerful knowledge and skills is increasing. Employer bodies such as the CBI have stressed that skills must have a much more central place in our education system. Reporting that 44% of employers find that young people leaving school, college and university are unready for the world of work, the CBI is advocating for character and broader skills, from team leadership to problem-solving, to be much further embedded in the curriculum. In a survey, the CBI found that 47% of teachers felt there were fewer opportunities to develop these skills and competencies owing to changes to GCSEs and A levels, 'citing a new focus on rote learning as a detriment to developing the skills and attitudes needed for work'.[91]

Of course, in any sensible education debate, knowledge and skills would simply not be polar opposites. As Schleicher explains: 'Of course, state-of-the-art knowledge will always remain important. Innovative or creative people generally have specialised skills in a specific field of knowledge or practice. As much as learning-to-learn skills are important, we always learn by learning something.'[92] But he adds the centrally important caveat: knowledge is not enough. 'Educational success is no longer primarily about reproducing content knowledge, but rather about extrapolating from what we know and applying that knowledge creatively in novel situations,' Schleicher argues.[93]

In contrast to Schleicher's dynamic concept of learning, Hirsch and his advocates barely engage with the crucial question of how children learn. They view knowledge as a fixed entity to be transmitted to pupils who must receive it and learn it before they can make any use of it. In the Hirschian model, knowledge is inert, fixed, stable – ready to be delivered, more like a sack of potatoes than a box of delights, to the next generation. In life, though, even in the rarefied world of academia, knowledge isn't like this at all. It is dynamic, shifting, uncertain, argued over. It is the stuff of debate and uncertainty, not of lists and certitudes.[94]

TO CONCLUDE

The last section of this chapter has sought to explore why a curriculum based on powerful knowledge has not delivered a transformation in the educational and vocational achievements of poor young people in relation to their wealthier peers. It has sought to confront the uncomfortable truth: that the attainment gap is now widening.

To tie together the ends of a disparate chapter, I will finish with this. The extent and severity of child poverty in England, and its savage effect on poor children's educational attainment, is too great an obstacle for educators to overcome – and a powerful knowledge curriculum is not up to the huge scale of the challenge when faced with the current epidemic of child poverty.

Children who come to school hungry, cold and distressed by the cruel miseries inflicted on them find it far harder to learn. The most able, or the luckiest, will escape the circumstances of their birth. But why should we require those children who have the worst start in life to jump the biggest hurdles to escape their conditions? Why are teachers persistently blamed for the economic inequality in our society that blights poor children and young people's early lives and, too often, their adult futures? Throughout the world, societies that are more equal in economic terms are more equal in educational achievement. Until politicians and the public join the dots we will continue to look for answers – in the curriculum or in the mirage of a better teaching workforce – that will not answer the question.

CHAPTER 5.
A SHORT HISTORY OF GOVERNMENT INCOMPETENCE IN EDUCATION POLICYMAKING

Ministers may be reluctant to reform Ofsted but they show no such reticence when it comes to their own reforming zeal. There have been more than 80 government acts relating to education since 1979, so education has gone through three times more legislation than health and five times more than defence.[95]

The explosion of education legislation has been matched by increasingly short ministerial lives. In the past 40 years there have been 20 education secretaries and more than 100 education ministers, each keen to make their mark and leave a lasting impression. The result has been education policymaking that is short-term, hugely contested and highly uncertain in its effect. Given that it takes three to five years for education changes to 'bed down' in the system, the consequences for teachers of this frenetic governmental action are significant and will be explored in this chapter.

Since the mid-1980s, with the advent of GCSEs, policy churn has been the norm for the Department for Education. Perhaps the best example of the very different aims for education held by the two main political parties can be seen in the frequent changes of name for this department. In 1992, the Department of Education and Science was renamed the Department for Education (DfE). In 1995, it was merged with the Department for Employment to become the Department for Education and Employment. In 2001, it was renamed the Department for Education and Skills (DfES) to signal the New Labour government's intention to increase national productivity through skills development. In 2007, the DfES was renamed the Department for Children, Schools and Families (DCSF) to signal the policy direction of the rather older 'New' Labour government, which culminated in the Extended Schools agenda – with schools as hubs for child development and parental support, particularly in disadvantaged areas. With the election of the coalition government in 2010, the DCSF returned to its 1992 name, the Department for Education, with a strong refocusing of the concept of the school as an academic institution that exists to provide education, not child development and parental support.

It was not always so. The Department for Education was traditionally viewed as a backwater where ministers would have little to do. A radical change in attitude was signalled by Prime Minister Jim Callaghan's 1976 speech to Ruskin College, Oxford, which began the long journey away from high-level oversight of the education system to the current reality of ministerial micromanagement. Callaghan had, in today's terms, very limited ambitions. He argued that it was wrong that 'the purpose of education should not have public attention focused on it'; that no one sector had exclusive rights in determining education policy and practice; that public interest 'is strong and legitimate and will be satisfied'; that 'parents, teachers, learned and professional bodies, representatives of higher education and both sides of industry, together with the government, all have an important part to play in formulating and expressing the purpose of education and the standards that we need'.

Viewed from the present, Callaghan's speech is remarkable for the breadth of his legitimate education stakeholders. The range is far, far narrower today. Government ministers have accreted to themselves huge powers, including the right to decide what is taught in schools and how it is assessed, with only the most perfunctory 'consultation' with stakeholders, including teachers, and with almost complete impunity to ignore any 'consultation' that does not align with pre-established ministerial viewpoints and direction of travel.

The 2010 formation of the Conservative/Liberal Democrat coalition and the appointment of Michael Gove as education secretary led to the biggest reform of compulsory education since the 1944 Education Act. The Academies Act 2010 – flying under the radar as health reforms absorbed all the political attention and oxygen, and introduced under an emergency legislation timetable – allowed all schools to become academies. The act set in train huge structural change in the organisation of schools, the demise of local authorities and the growth of multi-academy trusts.

Structural reform of schools through academisation was accompanied by equally ambitious reform of the curriculum, assessment and qualifications. Using the metaphorical sword of 'freedom' for teachers, Gove embarked on a highly ideological and radically political reform of the national curriculum, accompanied by fundamental revision of the national assessment arrangements for primary pupils and fundamental qualification change at GCSE and A level.

Characteristically, Gove did not hesitate to use – and indeed he relished – the rhetoric of battle. He used the tried-and-tested tactic of claiming a crisis (in this case the demise of education standards in England) to make the case for radical change. In *The Importance of Teaching*, the white paper that introduced the coalition government's education reforms, the case was trenchantly made:

> *'Our school system performs well below its potential and can improve significantly … Many other countries have much smaller gaps between the achievements of rich and poor than we do. The very best performing education systems show us that there need be no contradiction between a rigorous focus on high standards and a determination to narrow attainment gaps between pupils from different parts of society; between a rigorous and stretching curriculum and high participation in education; or between autonomous teachers and schools and high levels of accountability.'*[96]

Ministerial grabs for power and control were very cleverly hidden. The confident assertions that teachers would be 'autonomous' were bolstered by the frequent repetition of 'freedom'. The word is used 41 times in *The Importance of Teaching*, and 'autonomy' 36 times. Teachers were to be 'freed' from constraint. Their professional status was to be 'improved'. They were to have 'renewed authority'. Their status was to be 'raised'. Headteachers were to be freed from the requirement to 'comply with the wishes of government'. A brave new world of professional respect and autonomy was promised to the profession.

The main vehicle to achieve the unshackling of teachers and headteachers was the reform of the national curriculum, its assessment at primary level and the radical reform of GCSEs and A levels. Here, a gold standard of 'the best internationally' was set. The national curriculum would become a 'benchmark outlining the knowledge and concepts pupils should be expected to master to take their place as educated members of society'.

Driving all these changes was the concept of 'powerful' knowledge, explored in chapter 4. Ministers used this concept to signal their aim for education to be a force to 'level up' the nation's children (although the term 'level up' was not in use in 2010). Poor children had the right, as much as their wealthier peers, to be taught the 'best which has been thought and said'.[97] Strongly influenced by the American education thinker ED Hirsch Jr, Gove and the schools minister, Nick Gibb, set about constructing a curriculum and assessment system that would inculcate in all children and young people the powerful knowledge they would need to compete in the world. This knowledge was no longer to be the preserve of the rich. A shared cultural inheritance would bind our society together, enabling poor children to overcome the accident of their birth and become upwardly socially mobile.

Thus followed a frenzied period of educational legislation, summarised below.

2010	Coalition government publishes *The Importance of Teaching*, the schools white paper that confirms plans to reform the national curriculum, slimming down content and reducing prescription, and to 'seek advice' from Ofqual on changes to 'restore confidence' in GCSEs.
National curriculum reform	
2011	The Education Act 2011 abolishes the Qualifications and Curriculum Development Agency and puts no similar authority in its place. As a consequence, the education secretary may now make changes to the curriculum 'by order' (a kind of statutory instrument) without referring their proposal to an independent authority. Although the education secretary must give notice of the proposal to key stakeholders, an independent authority no longer decides who those stakeholders are; stakeholders are now those who 'appear to the Secretary of State to be concerned with the proposal'.
January 2011	Department for Education announces a review of the national curriculum and establishes expert panel to advise.

December 2011	Expert panel report published and timetable for implementation of new curriculum altered – first teaching of core subjects delayed until September 2014.
June 2012	Publication of draft programmes of study for English, maths and science at KS1 and KS2.
February 2013	Publication of further draft programmes of study in foundation subjects (but not English, maths and science at KS4).
September 2013	Publication of final national curriculum and programmes of study for teaching from September 2014.
December 2013	Publication of programmes of study for English, maths and science at KS4.
Primary assessment reform	
June 2011	Government commissions Lord Bew to review KS2 assessment arrangements and the role of SATs. Bew recommends the end of the use of national curriculum levels.
June 2012	Phonics screening check becomes mandatory for pupils at the end of Year 1.
July 2013	Government publishes proposals for primary assessment and accountability arrangements for the new national curriculum. This confirms the intention to scrap national curriculum levels.
March 2014	Government response to consultation on its primary school assessment and accountability proposals: introduction of a baseline Reception test for four-year-olds; a phonics test near the end of Year 1; teacher assessment at the end of KS1 in maths, reading and writing, speaking and listening, and science; national tests at the end of KS2 in maths, reading, grammar, punctuation and spelling, and teacher assessment of maths, reading, writing and science.
February 2015	Commission on 'assessment without levels'.
September 2015	Introduction of Reception baseline. Standards and Testing Agency issues guidance on teacher assessment at KS1 and KS2.
November 2015	Education secretary Nicky Morgan announces plans to require students to resit SATs if they don't meet the expected level at KS2.
February 2016	Standards and Testing Agency publishes sample exemplification materials for teacher assessment.
April 2016	Reception baseline abandoned because of comparability problems with three providers.
Summer term 2016	First KS1 and KS2 national assessments based on revised national curriculum.
September 2021	Reception baseline assessment made statutory in all schools.

Secondary assessment reform	
September 2012	Education secretary Michael Gove makes a statement in the House of Commons announcing the government's intention to replace GCSEs with new qualifications called English Baccalaureate Certificates (EBCs), which would cover the core academic subjects that form the English Baccalaureate: English, maths, sciences, history, geography and languages. Gove also proposes a single awarding body organisation in each subject for a period of five years. The Department for Education launches a consultation on reforming KS4 qualifications. Consultation closes on 10 December 2012.
16 January 2013	Opposition Day debate on exam reform: MPs express strong concerns about the content and implementation of the proposed EBCs. In particular there is concern about the treatment of creative subjects and the single awarding system.
7 February 2013	Gove announces he will not be pursuing a single exam board for each academic subject; English EBCs will not be introduced and existing GCSEs will be reformed. In order to address grade inflation, dumbing down and the loss of rigour in GCSEs and A levels, these exams will be reformed 'with the help of school and university leaders'. The qualifications will be linear, with all assessments normally taken at the end of the course. Ofqual is sent a 'policy steer' letter on GCSEs in which Gove writes: 'Internal assessment and the use of exam aids should be kept to a minimum and used only where there is a compelling case to do so, to provide for effective and deep assessment of the specified curriculum content.'
February – May 2013	Consultation on school accountability measures at KS4.
June 2013	Ofqual publishes GCSE reform consultation: 'We propose that where subject content can be validly assessed by written exams, such exams set and marked by exam boards should be the default method of assessment.'
September 2013	Performance measures for schools changed to deter early entry to GCSEs.
October 2013	Announcement on Progress 8 as the new accountability measure at KS4. This measure will be introduced for all schools in 2016 based on 2016 GCSE exam results measured across the English Baccalaureate subjects – English, maths, sciences, computer science, geography, history and languages – and three further subjects.

1 November 2013	Ofqual publishes a suite of documents, including an analysis of the responses to the June consultation and information on how the reforms will subsequently proceed. An Ofqual press notice, 'Design details of new GCSEs in England', announces the key features of the new GCSEs:
	• A new grading scale that uses the numbers 1-9 to identify levels of performance, with 9 being the top level.
	• A fully linear structure with all assessment at the end of the course and content not divided into modules.
	• Exams as the default method of assessment.
	• Summer exams.
	• The timetable for the introduction of new GCSEs is altered. English literature, English language and maths are to be introduced from September 2015, with the new GCSEs in other subjects to be introduced from the following year. (Previously all were intended to be introduced from September 2015.)
April 2014	Ofqual issues a new consultation document, *Consultation on Setting the Grade Standards of New GCSEs in England*. The consultation closes on 30 June 2014.
September 2014	Ofqual publishes its response to the consultation on the new grading system, confirming that new GCSEs will be graded 1-9. Under the revised system, according to Ofqual, broadly the same proportion of students will achieve a grade 4 and above as currently achieve a grade C and above. Grade 5 will be positioned in the top third of the marks for a current grade C and the bottom third of the marks for a current Grade B – broadly in line with the average performance of high-performing education nations in the OECD's Programme for International Student Assessment (PISA). The new system will be in place from September 2015 for students receiving their results in 2017.
16 June 2015	Education secretary Nicky Morgan announces that the new GCSE grading system will set a new level of what constitutes a 'good pass'. The existing system of using grade C as the base measure will be altered to the new grade 5. Grade 5 will be the equivalent of a high C or low B under the existing system, whereas the bottom of the current grade C will be the bottom of the new grade 4. The government states that this will bring the standard in line with top-performing education nations.
28 March 2017	Education secretary Justine Greening writes to the chair of the Education Select Committee revising Morgan's 16 June 2015 announcement. Now grade 4 is a standard pass: where employers, FE providers and universities currently accept a grade C, they are now expected to continue recognising a grade 4. Grade 5 is a strong pass.

Seen like this, the scale and extent of the changes made to the curriculum and its assessment become clear. Just reading the chart is exhausting. The prospect of change, bolstered by consultation documents, rained down relentlessly on teachers and leaders who were working the most unpaid overtime of any profession, and had little or no time to read the hundreds of pages of consultation documents that preceded the revised curriculum programmes of study and the new GCSE and A level qualification requirements.

I made this point repeatedly to government ministers in this period and in particular to Gibb, with whom I had a good working relationship despite my profound disagreements with the policy he was pursing. He would readily agree that the pace of change was, in his words, 'punishing' to the profession, but would then assure me that once we had got through this rough period, with the new curriculum and qualifications in place, things would 'settle down' and teachers could move into the sunny uplands of freedom and autonomy.

I thought the minister's reply displayed a startling ignorance of the reality of the situation for teachers. Each and every minor change in a national curriculum document results in hours and hours of work, as teachers revise their schemes of work, lesson plans and assessments. But these changes were *major* – in some cases involving an almost complete rewrite of the national curriculum programme of study – with huge consequences for teachers. They had to master the new fields of required knowledge and then consider how to teach them: what sources to use, what would be the best pedagogical approach and how to assess. And remember that teachers were given no reduction in their teaching time to adapt to these profound changes. All the work to acquaint themselves with the demands of the new curriculum at primary and secondary level (and remember that primary teachers had to cover all 10 national curriculum subjects), the new syllabuses at GCSE and A level, and the move to end-of-course timed exams was completed in their own time, on top of full teaching workloads.

LOST IN THE FOG OF REFORM

It is important to note that there was no consensus about the reforms. In fact, they were highly controversial and hotly contested. One of many public spats illustrates this point well. Having been appointed to the government's 'expert panel' to advise on the revision of the national curriculum, Andrew Pollard, upon seeing the proposed programmes of study, broke cover and asked: 'What about the pupils?' In an explosive blog post published in 2012, Pollard argued that the government's approach was 'fatally flawed'. He wrote that although subject knowledge was important, and that emphasis on English grammar and spelling was likely to be highly attractive to the public, the reforms would fail without 'parallel consideration of the needs of learners'.[98]

In direct opposition to the government's claims that the new curriculum would 'free' teachers to teach, Pollard argued that the very detailed year-on-year specifications in the core subjects of maths, English and science, 'complemented by punitive inspection arrangements and tough new tests at 11', would constrain the primary curriculum and deny teachers the opportunity to exercise their professional knowledge and experience. Pollard wrote:

> *'The skill and expertise of the teacher lies in building on each pupil's existing understanding and capabilities, and in matching tasks to extend attainment. To do these things, they need scope to exercise professional judgement.'*

Gove took up the cudgels in his response, which was published, appropriately, in *The Daily Mail*.[99] Never one to resist fanning the flames, Gove called Pollard and the 100 academics who signed a letter to *The Independent* newspaper, protesting about the changes to the national curriculum, the 'new enemies of promise' and accused them of 'actively trying to prevent millions of our poorest children getting the education they need'. Ever a fan of the rhetorical question, Gove asked: 'What planet are these people on?' He trashed the work of teachers, maintaining that standards in science had been 'so dumbed down that children could be asked if grilled fish is healthier than battered sausages in their GCSEs'. (Given the scale of childhood obesity in the UK, on the rise and dangerously a marker for poor adult health on an industrial scale, this question seems remarkably apposite to me.)

It was not only the nature but also the pace of the reform that led to severe problems for teachers and leaders. One significant change was the replacement of the established alphabetical A-G GCSE grading system with a numerical system of 1-9 – with 9, counterintuitively, the top grade. But no one could tell teachers, as they embarked upon teaching the new GCSEs, what was the numerical equivalent of a grade C. Remarkably, it took the government three goes, in 2014, 2015 and 2017, to determine the equivalence between a grade C and levels 4 and 5 of the new grading system. That fact, more than anything else, is testimony to this overly hasty and poorly implemented reform. The government's startling inability to answer this basic, fundamental question caused teachers taking GCSE classes immense stress. They felt, rightly, that they were not able to give their pupils accurate feedback about the standards they were achieving and their predicted grades – information that young people need in order to consider and plan their post-16 options. Employers were also at a loss as to what the new grading system meant.

In August 2017, a highly successful headteacher complained to me of the chronic uncertainty about the new GCSE levels, asking despairingly: 'What does a grade 7, 8 or 9 look like?' He confirmed that teachers were working in the dark and were having to make up their own assessment systems. The headteacher confessed that he had 'no idea of progress in maths and English in his school' and was worried about the amount of teachers' time that was devoted to trying to do things well without the requisite information or tools. He told me: 'My teachers are slogging their way through a confused system and it's knocking out of school time anything to do with school quality.'

Mired in confusion, this must be one of the most chaotic 'reforms' in educational history.

Similar chaos affected primary teachers taking Year 6 classes. The Standards and Testing Agency's first set of guidance for the 2016 key stage 2 teacher assessment of writing was withdrawn in September 2015 because it was found to be unworkable. If a Year 6 teacher with a class of 30 pupils had followed the instructions in the KS2 writing assessment guidance, they would have had to undertake more than 6,000 assessments based on 34 assessment statements across six examples of pupils' work. A second set of guidance arrived in late February 2016. This was similarly unworkable and was followed by no fewer than five 'clarifications' of the guidance issued, followed by a further 13 updated documents released on 24 March 2016 – the last day of term, 16 days after the previous 'clarification'.[100]

The government incompetence caused by the breakneck speed of the reform led teachers to despair. It is difficult to think of any profession other than teaching that would have been subject to this level of incompetence. Teachers felt they were being treated with contempt as their professional knowledge and expertise, their sense of what was likely to work and what was not, were swept away by the tide of change and ignored by politicians convinced that they knew best.

EMPTY PROMISES

All this might have been forgiven (although insults to the profession on that scale are remembered and continue to rankle) if the promise of freedom and autonomy had been realised. But it was not.

One of the key promises made to teachers by ministers was that the move away from modularised assessment at GCSE and A level, along with the decoupling of AS and A level, would liberate teachers and pupils from the pressure of continual assessment throughout the course. There would, ministers confidently asserted, be more time for teachers to teach and to explore in-depth mastery of their subject.

Sadly, the bright future assured by Gove and Gibb did not materialise. A survey of secondary teachers in 2016, a year into the new qualifications, revealed that more than three-quarters of teachers of English and maths (the subjects constituting the first wave of the new GCSEs) strongly agreed that their classroom practice had become more focused on exam and test preparation.[101] One spoke for many when she commented:

> *'The sheer level of fear about accountability and the difficulty of the new GCSEs and of terminal assessments have meant the ENTIRE curriculum from Y7 has been reduced to replicated GCSE style assessment. Kids are doing far more testing. The curriculum has narrowed. Forms of assessment have become narrowed. Teaching is becoming more a form of 'transmission'. It is depressing. Kids feel fatigued and stressed. I feel bored and demotivated.'*

Teachers of other subjects had similar concerns, with 87% agreeing that their classroom practice would become more focused on exam and test preparation. Teachers complained of the increased content of the revised syllabuses, making it a 'race' to cover it in the teaching time available. Concern was expressed that key concepts in a subject would be 'skimmed' and, paradoxically, the curriculum 'narrowed' in order to cover the topics to be examined.

Importantly – and embarrassingly for government ministers – teachers' perceptions that, far from being 'autonomous' and 'free', they were in fact confined and constrained by teaching to the test were confirmed by the OECD. In a presentation to the 2016 International Summit on the Teaching Profession, the OECD's head of education, Andreas Schleicher, presented a slide that put the English education system at the top of the OECD league table for rote learning, and bottom for the promotion of 'deep learning' involving complex cognitive activation strategies.

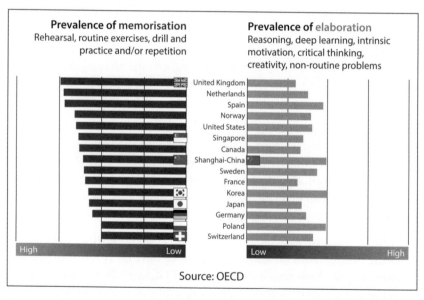

Source: OECD

I was in the room during this presentation and took the opportunity to ask Schleicher why England's education system was at such extreme ends – so high on memorisation and so low on deep thinking. He answered with a rhetorical question: 'Exams focus on the reproduction of subject knowledge content, so why would teachers invest in cognitive elaboration strategies?' Schleicher emphasised the need for students to be able to think creatively and critically, to assimilate information from a range of sources, to refocus information towards a new purpose or to solve a different problem, to communicate well, to evaluate sources of information and data, to have good IT skills, to be able to recognise fake news, and to have the interpersonal skills of empathy, communication and collaboration. All these were becoming increasingly essential for fulfilled individual lives and for the productivity and success of nations. The problem, Schleicher asserted, was the English education system's over-reliance on exams that demand the reproduction of learned content, and the lack of time and opportunity for students to engage in more open-ended tasks that require the transformation of knowledge across subject disciplines in order to solve complex real-life problems.

Further evidence that the coalition government's reforms had accomplished the exact opposite of its stated intentions was revealed in the OECD's TALIS 2018. The OECD was clear about the importance of teacher autonomy, stating that the extent to which teachers were able to make decisions in their work had been identified as a cornerstone of teacher professionalism. It argued that teacher autonomy should be realised by giving teachers more control over the core aspects of their work, such as determining course content or choosing learning materials. But TALIS revealed that England's education system performed very poorly for teacher autonomy, coming third from the bottom of the OECD league table for teachers who 'agreed or strongly agreed' that they had control over determining 'course content', by which is meant the curriculum and teaching and learning approaches for their classes.[102] England was also below the OECD average for teachers reporting that they were able to innovate in their teaching and collaborate professionally.

The chasm between the government's stated aims for the profession and the lived reality of teachers could not be wider. The DfE's 2017 analysis of factors relating to teacher supply found that the scale and pace of government education reform came second only to workload as the reason given for leaving teaching.[103] As they bade farewell to the classroom, those teachers who were leaving the profession clearly did not agree that they had been given professional status, freedom and autonomy.

Gove was sacked as education secretary in 2014 on the advice of the Tories' election strategist, Lynton Crosby, who advised the then prime minister, David Cameron, that Gove had become 'toxic' to the electorate. Gove has since moved on to other things, which are not the subject of this book. His legacy, in terms of the standing of the DfE and his successors, is increasingly contested.

Faced with the Covid-19 pandemic and the closure of schools to most pupils for prolonged periods throughout 2020 and 2021, the DfE has been exposed as a weak link mistrusted by No. 10 and the Treasury. So much so that decisions about school openings and closures were routinely made without DfE involvement and even without the involvement of Gavin Williamson, the hapless education secretary throughout this period.

The DfE is a department with poor institutional memory and with fundamentally inadequate methods of communicating with schools, whether they are academies or local authority-maintained. Fuelled by ideological hatred of LAs, which ministers fervently believed were 'stuffed full of progressives who do not believe in phonics',[104] the government resorted repeatedly to command and control tactics, issuing orders and guidance that were contradictory and constantly changed – rather than opting for the eminently sensible alternative of using the 150 LAs to coordinate communications to the schools in their area. This hugely and unnecessarily increased the workload of school leaders, who were struggling to do the right thing for their pupils and their staff during a lethal pandemic.[105] The Institute for Government reports:

> 'Between mid-March and the end of May 2020 no fewer than 148 new guidance documents, or updates to existing material, were issued to schools. Much of it was published at the end of a week or late in the evening, according to the NAO, "putting schools under pressure, especially when guidance was for immediate implementation". In addition, "when the guidance was updated, schools were not always clear what changes had been made".'[106]

The despair of school leaders at the DfE's appalling ineptitude was clear for all to see. It played out as they expressed their rage at the arrival in their email inbox, late in the evening, of updated versions of guidance, frequently 40 or 50 pages long, without tracked changes. Some kindly souls took to Twitter to signal the points and pages in different versions where the text had been changed.

Williamson ploughed ever deeper furrows, proclaiming that he was in control of events when he was not. He asserted that the algorithm that determined the grades awarded for the 2020 GCSE and A level exams was the fairest means of assessing pupils, until he had to concede that it was not. The algorithm transformed, according to Prime Minister Boris Johnson, from 'world-beating' to 'mutant', resulting in its abandonment in favour of centre-assessed grades. Learning nothing from this humiliating experience, the saga was repeated the following year. Despite increasing evidence of rising infection in schools and in the community, Williamson insisted that exams would take place come what may – until, on 6 January 2021, he was forced to the House of Commons to admit that this would not, in fact, be the case. Instead, teacher-assessed grades would be used for GCSEs and A levels, leaving teachers and leaders to pick up the pieces, under increased workload and stress, of Williamson's failure to plan ahead and to consider carefully the unpalatable but obvious truth that schools might have to close in 2021 as they did in 2020.

A DEPARTMENT ISOLATED, MISTRUSTED AND DETACHED

There can be no doubt that Williamson made a bad situation worse through his incompetence and ignorance. Equally, there can be no doubt that the DfE was unable to support its secretary of state because the communication links it had with LAs were broken, and because regional commissioners – whose role is to provide oversight of academies and multi-academy trusts in their areas – were unable to coordinate and communicate effectively with the 8,700 schools with which they had very limited and ineffective working relationships. Government ministers' determination to bypass and ignore LAs and to rely on regional commissioners during the pandemic revealed just how ineffective is the 'middle tier' between central government and schools in England, without the human or financial resources to provide either the support that school leaders so desperately needed, or the feedback to central government on what was actually happening in schools during this intense, fast-moving and hugely stressful period.

As someone closely involved in stakeholder engagement with the DfE and with government education ministers during the pandemic, I can attest to the frequent incredulity expressed by stakeholders after meetings with ministers and civil servants. They seemed to exist in an alternate universe where 'it would be all right on the night'. Warnings and advice from stakeholders were ignored, with the inevitable consequence that the worst outcomes were, in fact, realised time after time – to the huge detriment of pupils, their parents and education professionals.

Covid-19 has brutally exposed the government's lack of effective oversight and management of the education system. It has laid bare, for all to see, a Department for Education that is unable to communicate effectively with school leaders either in normal times or in a crisis. The DfE's huge powers over the curriculum, qualifications and assessment, taken from previously independent government agencies, are exercised incompetently – as demonstrated by the history of curriculum and assessment reform since 2010, and by the 2020 and 2021 fiascos over GCSEs and A level grades. The department is isolated within government, mistrusted by No. 10 and unable to exert leverage on the Treasury, which turns a deaf ear to the DfE's case for increased education funding for the catch-up recovery programmes so desperately needed by the poorest and most deprived children and young people. The DfE is also detached from the workforce it is meant to serve. Astonishingly, 74% of NEU members think the DfE is run in a way to undermine teachers, while 82% think the DfE has a negative impact on what happens in their classrooms.[107]

All this is true despite the many DfE officials that I have worked with who are expert, knowledgeable and very hardworking. They want to do a good job. They know the department's capacity to communicate with its stakeholders, and in particular school leaders, is weak and want to do something about it. They do the best they can, acting as professionally as possible under the often misguided and wrong-headed direction of their political masters.

Shakespeare knew that reputation, once lost, cannot be regained. Government ministers and the DfE are distrusted and despised by teachers and leaders who feel they are not cared for by those who should be their guardians and champions. After Covid-19, the DfE's epitaph might be: 'It is a tale told by an idiot, full of sound and fury, signifying nothing.'[108]

CHAPTER 6.
A BETTER DEAL FOR TEACHERS STARTS HERE

I have spent much of this book making the strongest case I can that if we are to rescue teaching as an attractive profession – one in which more than 60% of its members are willing to remain for longer than 10 years – then we must take radical action. By 'we' I mean government, the profession itself (teachers and school leaders) and wider society (including employers and parents). Achieving change will not be easy, nor will it be quick. It's a hard road to travel but the journey must begin somewhere – so let's start here.

But before we consider the ways in which the working lives of teachers might be improved, let us consider whether this book's critique of the current professional working environment for teachers, and the forces that have created it, is shared more generally in the profession. Are the arguments I have made in the previous chapters the impassioned but wrong-headed musings of an education trade union leader? Or do they articulate and develop the serious concerns felt by teachers about the state of the schools they work in and the effect of national education policy on the quality of their working lives?

Recent and ongoing research by the DfE, I am pleased to report, supports and reinforces the arguments I have made and the concerns I have expressed in this book. More than 1,000 school leaders were asked what wider system changes were needed in education to support recovery from the longer-term impacts of the Covid-19 pandemic on teaching and learning.[109] The results are reproduced in the following chart.

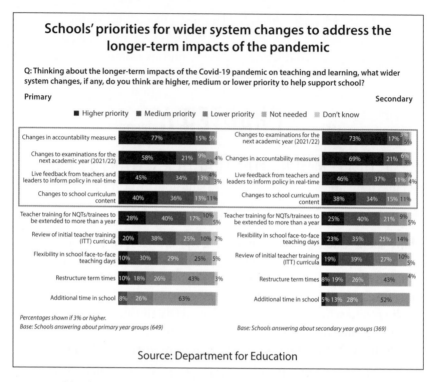

Schools' priorities for wider system changes to address the longer-term impacts of the pandemic

Q: Thinking about the longer-term impacts of the Covid-19 pandemic on teaching and learning, what wider system changes, if any, do you think are higher, medium or lower priority to help support school?

Primary   **Secondary**

■ Higher priority   ■ Medium priority   ■ Lower priority   ■ Not needed   ■ Don't know

Primary		Secondary	
Changes in accountability measures	77% / 15% / 5%	Changes to examinations for the next academic year (2021/22)	73% / 17% / 3% / 5%
Changes to examinations for the next academic year (2021/22)	58% / 21% / 9% / 8% / 4%	Changes in accountability measures	69% / 21% / 6% / 3%
Live feedback from teachers and leaders to inform policy in real-time	45% / 34% / 13% / 4% / 3%	Live feedback from teachers and leaders to inform policy in real-time	46% / 37% / 11% / 3% / 4%
Changes to school curriculum content	40% / 36% / 13% / 11%	Changes to school curriculum content	38% / 34% / 15% / 11%
Teacher training for NQTs/trainees to be extended to more than a year	28% / 40% / 17% / 10% / 5%	Teacher training for NQTs/trainees to be extended to more than a year	25% / 40% / 21% / 9% / 5%
Review of initial teacher training (ITT) curricula	20% / 38% / 25% / 10% / 7%	Flexibility in school face-to-face teaching days	23% / 35% / 25% / 14%
Flexibility in school face-to-face teaching days	10% / 30% / 29% / 25% / 5%	Review of initial teacher training (ITT) curricula	19% / 39% / 27% / 10% / 5%
Restructure term times	10% / 18% / 26% / 43% / 3%	Restructure term times	8% / 19% / 26% / 43% / 4%
Additional time in school	8% / 26% / 63%	Additional time in school	5% / 13% / 28% / 52%

Percentages shown if 3% or higher.
Base: Schools answering about primary year groups (649)   *Base: Schools answering about secondary year groups (369)*

Source: Department for Education

It is notable that the two top priorities, in reverse order for primary and secondary schools, are 'Changes in accountability measures' and 'Changes to examinations for the next academic year (2021/22)'. The survey findings were further explored by the researchers through more than 40 interviews with school leaders. When talking about changes to accountability measures (a high priority for 77% of primaries and 73% of secondaries), leaders referred to revision of Ofsted's inspection criteria, approach and process.

School leaders discussed the uncertainties around Ofsted. They were concerned about Ofsted inspections and judgements that 'may not adequately recognise the complex challenges faced by pupils and schools following the pandemic and extended home-schooling'.[110] One primary school leader is reported as saying: 'I am concerned that those schools that bust a gut in order to make sure those children are mentally stable in order to access learning – that could be misconstrued as a school not having high expectations of their children in terms of learning.'[111]

Primary and secondary leaders identified changes to exams as either their first (secondary schools) or their second (primary schools) priority. Although the research does not elaborate on this response, I take this to mean that leaders want changes that would compensate for the loss of face-to-face teaching time and gaps in pupil learning caused by absence and/or inability to access remote learning during lockdown. One secondary school leader asked: 'Can we do assessment differently to have a better world class system – can we take the positives and work together for something better, more resilient?'[112]

Notable, too, are school leaders' third and fourth priorities. Their third priority is 'Live feedback from teachers and leaders to inform policy in real-time', which I think speaks to the disconnect and dislocation the profession has felt from government and the 'uplifting' ministerial announcements that appear to reveal little or no understanding of the pressured and draining reality of school life during the pandemic. Leaders, responsible for the health and safety of their staff and their pupils, have felt frustrated and let down because of the last-minute and frequently changing guidance issued without track changes.

The fourth priority for primary and secondary leaders is 'Changes to school curriculum content'. This priority receives no further elaboration in the DfE research, which is surprising given that the DfE is in the process of conducting a national curriculum review. Surely this evidence of the profession's view of the curriculum and its appropriateness should be fully and adequately reported and taken into consideration by the DfE as it conducts its review? It is, after all, the DfE's own research that has produced these findings.

Of course, it is a good thing that ministers and civil servants in the DfE have asked school leaders for their views. The profession needs more of this. What is concerning, however, is that although these views are summarily reported, there is no indication that ministers or their civil servants are going to do anything about the issues identified by leaders as key to their school's recovery from the effects of the pandemic.

I am saddened by this, but I am not surprised. The four priorities identified by leaders – changes in accountability measures, changes to exams, feedback from the profession to inform government policy, and changes to school curriculum content – are, without doubt, going to be put into the 'too difficult' folder and locked away in the DfE filing cabinet. The strongest evidence of this is that, far from considering what changes to the accountability regime are needed because of the effects of the pandemic on pupil experiences and learning, Ofsted inspections have resumed with the 2019 inspection framework – and at a time when levels of Covid infection among primary pupils are growing exponentially, further disrupting any return to 'normal' in schools. How the judgements made by the inspectorate can reliably and validly express the quality of education provided by schools in these extraordinary and unprecedented times is anyone's guess.

Primary SATs and secondary GCSE and A level exams are returning for 2022, with inadequate mitigations for the disruption to pupils' learning and, for the secondary public exams, with grade thresholds that are raised and will result in lower grades for the pupils whose learning has been most disrupted during the three academic years of the pandemic.

We cannot, I am afraid, leave it to government ministers – or to the civil servants at the DfE acting under their policy direction – to do the fundamental thinking required to change the English education system in ways that are absolutely necessary to the pupils it serves and the teachers it relies so heavily upon. That being the case, this chapter contains a series of modest proposals for what could be done to bring about change for the better.

The NEU recently asked teachers what they wanted from their working lives. It's a question that is too rarely asked: the more usual formulation is 'What don't you want from your working lives?' or 'What is driving you from the profession?' Teachers' responses were organised by the time they had spent in the profession and are detailed in the following chart.

Time as fully qualified teacher (FQT): 1-2 years		Time as FQT: 3-5 years		Time as FQT: 6-15 years		Time as FQT: 16+ years	
Educators receiving a pay rise to reflect the work they do	69%	Educators receiving a pay rise to reflect the work they do	64%	How teachers' professional time is managed	47%	How teacher professionalism is recognised and managed	49%
How teacher professionalism is recognised and managed	40%	How teachers' professional time is managed	50%	Educators receiving a pay rise to reflect the work they do	45%	Educators receiving a pay rise to reflect the work they do	45%
Ensuring there is adequate development for support staff	34%	Having more flexible working lives	38%	How teacher professionalism is recognised and managed	41%	How teachers' professional time is managed	39%
Having a professional pay, appraisal and career development policy	29%	How teacher professionalism is recognised and managed	34%	Having more flexible working lives	39%	Having a professional approach to pedagogy and curriculum	36%
How teachers' professional time is managed	27%	Having a professional approach to pedagogy and curriculum	31%	Ensuring there is adequate development for support staff	32%	Ensuring there is adequate development for support staff	26%
Having a professional approach to pedagogy and curriculum	25%	Ensuring there is adequate development for support staff	23%	Having a professional approach to pedagogy and curriculum	28%	Having a professional pay, appraisal and career development policy	25%
Having more flexible working lives	24%	Having a professional pay, appraisal and career development policy	23%	Having a professional pay, appraisal and career development policy	26%	Having professional systems to cover teacher absence	24%
Having professional systems to cover teacher absence	15%	Having professional systems to cover teacher absence	18%	Having professional systems to cover teacher absence	20%	Having more flexible working lives	23%
None of them	6%	None of them	0%	None of them	0%	None of them	1%

Source: National Education Union

In this chapter, I discuss in turn each of the main concerns raised by teachers and one that has not been discussed previously: teachers' pay. I consider how teachers' time and professionalism could be better managed and what would be a sensible and informed approach to policy reform of pedagogy and curriculum. I will then present a plan for what to do about our failing inspectorate and what to do to improve the currently ineffective and inadequate government education policy reform.

TEACHERS' PAY

I have resisted writing about teachers' pay until now because I wanted to convey the depth and scale of the issues facing teachers more widely, and to confound the untrue perception that all union leaders talk about is pay. But pay cannot and should not be ignored. The chart on page 85 shows that pay is the most important issue for teachers in the first five years of their careers and remains a priority as they become more experienced. Teachers know they do essential work. They know how hard they work. They know that Covid-19 has revealed to parents and the public just how central their work is, not only in their essential role of teaching children and young people, but also in the social fabric of children's lives. In many communities, the school is the one public service still readily available to families in need.

A recent article from the Institute for Fiscal Studies (IFS), titled 'The long, long squeeze on teacher pay', does, as the title suggests, provide a compelling account of how teachers' pay has declined in real terms over the past 15 years.[113] The article notes that teachers' pay is important because it plays a big part in the recruitment and retention pressures faced by schools, which in turn determine the standard of education they are able to provide. The authors calculate that between 2007 and 2014 there was an 8% real-terms fall (including inflation as measured by CPI) in teacher pay levels – 1.5% more than the fall in general wages in this period.

The authors note that the government has responded to increasingly vocal concerns about teacher supply by targeting pay rises at newly qualified and beginning teachers. By September 2021 there had been a 5% real-terms rise in starting salaries; the bulk of this was due to a large rise in 2020, as part of the move towards the government's ambition of £30,000 starting salaries for teachers. Teachers in the earlier stages of their career

– on the main professional scale from M2 to M6 – have seen real-terms rises of 3-4%.

But more experienced teachers on the upper pay scale have seen their real-terms pay frozen between 2014 and 2021. This freeze affects more than half of all teachers. During the same period, average earnings in the wider economy rose by 7.5%. It is also notable that salaries for teachers in Scotland and Wales are now higher than those in England, by 7% and 5% respectively.

Of the discrepancy in pay growth between younger and more experienced teachers, the IFS article notes:

'Part of the motivation for this pattern of changes is the result of a desire to counteract falling retention rates for less experienced teachers and there is good evidence to suggest that younger, less experienced teachers are more sensitive to pay levels. However, forward thinking teachers will also make career decisions based on expected pay later in their career. More experienced teachers are, almost by definition, likely to have built up significant knowledge and experience, so any reduction in retention would represent a significant loss to schools.'[114]

Pay levels and prospects are not sufficiently attractive to prevent retention problems among experienced teachers as well as early career teachers. In England, the School Teachers' Review Body (STRB) noted that 'teachers' median earnings trailed the estimated median earnings of other professionals'.[115]

The challenge presented by declining retention rates is fully and starkly outlined in chapter 1 of this book. Increasing numbers of teachers are leaving just as they are gaining expertise in their practice, which leaves too many schools with too many inexperienced staff. Without the guidance that their more experienced colleagues could provide, these teachers buckle under the pressure and stress of the work and leave earlier and earlier in their careers.

It is a vicious cycle that causes huge problems for school leaders and the standards of education they can provide in their schools. Experience is invaluable in all walks of life and especially so in the complexity of teaching, where so much of the work is in the moment: in instant reactions to pupils' responses to learning and the expectations that teachers have of their behaviour. Experienced colleagues can ease the way of their more inexperienced peers, consoling them when they are having difficulties with their classes and pointing them towards what is important in their work. When this experienced cadre of teachers is hollowed out then the eager but inexperienced too often find that enthusiasm and commitment are not enough.

This turnover, of course, costs money. In the most recent report containing the relevant figures, the National Audit Office revealed that the DfE spent £555 million in 2013-14 on training and supporting beginning teachers.[116] That figure will be much bigger in 2021. How much less money would be wasted in the endless quest to replace teachers leaving the profession if they were paid properly in the first place? And not just at the start, but throughout their careers.

This is not, however, an argument that plays well with the Treasury. I vividly remember attending a meeting with David Gauke in 2016 when he was chief secretary to the Treasury. Despite all the evidence that I had ready to hand, Gauke calmly stated that the Treasury 'were not at all convinced' that there was a teacher supply crisis – a statement that had me, most unusually, lost for words. The government's own evidence to the STRB in February 2021, on the issue of the September 2021 pay award, noted that, despite the temporary improvement to teacher supply owing to the impact of the pandemic, 'the supply context remains challenging'.[117] The government's evidence also acknowledged that 'pay is a key driver for improving recruitment and retention'.

More recently, I was part of a TUC delegation to meet Chancellor Rishi Sunak at No. 11 Downing Street. I remonstrated with him in the meeting about the injustice of the current 'pay pause' for teachers, reminding him of the work teachers had done during the pandemic to reinvent themselves as remote educators, mastering new technology without any training in their efforts to keep the nation's children and young people engaged in learning. Sunak was unimpressed and became quite agitated. He compared the £38,000 median salary of teachers with the £24,000 median salary of other workers. He did not give me the chance to argue that this was not a fair comparison, because the majority of 'all other workers' will not have a degree and postgraduate qualification that will have delayed their earning potential. Nor are 'all other workers' subject to the excessive and intensive workload that teachers labour under.

The NEU submitted written evidence to the STRB in February 2021 setting out the key issues on teacher pay and demonstrating their impact on teacher supply. Government policy since 2010 – real-terms pay cuts, the dismantling of the national pay structure and the imposition of unfair performance-related pay – has contributed to the development of the major recruitment and retention crisis that is still playing out. The NEU's pay and progression survey has highlighted the inequalities created by the unfair pay system, with discriminatory outcomes evident. The key points raised by the NEU were also made by other STRB consultees on the September 2021 pay award, underlining the consensus on these issues.

The NEU evidence is clear. Teachers are acutely aware that their pay is not sufficient. They know that when they calculate the hours they work against their pay, they are working for less than the minimum wage. It is imperative that the government recognises the scale of the problem. Its ambitions for 'levelling up' cannot be achieved on the back of inadequate teacher supply, particularly because, as I show in chapter 4, this is a problem that disproportionately affects schools in disadvantaged areas.

FLEXIBLE WORKING

The chart of teacher priorities on page 85 presents a fascinating and complex picture of teachers' priorities at different stages of their careers. It is not surprising in a profession that is 76% female that 'having more flexible working lives' becomes a key priority for teachers after 3-5 years, when they will be thinking of starting a family, and remains a priority after 6-15 years, as they bring up young and very dependent children. The problem is that flexible working is not a characteristic of the teaching profession. I have lost count of the conversations I have had with female teachers with small children who have left the profession because their request to work two or three days a week was turned down.

Government ministers have championed flexible working and exhorted school leaders to adopt this practice, with little effect. And yet school leaders identify teacher shortages as their major impediment to raising educational standards. If they could embrace flexible working – recognising that women with young families find it impossible to balance the current workload demands of teaching with their childcare responsibilities, as women continue to shoulder the greater burden of childcare – then they would find their teacher supply problems much eased.

This book has not been kind to the DfE nor to government ministers, so let me redress that somewhat by recognising that the DfE has produced guidance and support for school leaders to promote flexible working. The guidance is aimed at helping employers to develop and implement flexible working policies, and to support employees who want to request flexible working.[118] It explains the benefits of this approach to retaining experienced staff, recruiting from a broader pool of talent, promoting wellbeing and improving work-life balance. It identifies specific groups of teachers who may benefit particularly, including those with caring responsibilities, those on phased returns to the profession, those returning from a career break and those who wish to combine their paid work with continuing professional development.

This is one piece of DfE guidance that I am happy to promote. Until we are able to change teachers' working lives to the point where it is possible to be a full-time teacher and a mother, flexible working can help to retain the experience, talent and professionalism of so many women. Flexible working would keep many more teachers in the profession, enabling them to further develop their expertise and to progress in their careers, and allowing them to share their experience with newly qualified and beginning teachers.

HOW TEACHERS' TIME AND PROFESSIONALISM ARE MANAGED

Although these are two separate categories on the chart, I take them to be two different ways of teachers saying the same thing. This book has provided ample and irrefutable evidence not only that teachers work excessive hours but also that their work is excessively intensive – they have too little control over it and too little say in how their work is evaluated. The chart on page 85 shows that teachers' lack of control over professional issues in which they are experienced and knowledgeable becomes more of a problem as they progress in their careers. The categories of time management and the recognition and management of their professionalism rise up the scale. As they become more experienced, teachers increasingly resent feeling that their working time is wasted in pointless bureaucracy. They feel this is a denial of their professionalism, because if it were truly valued then their views about how to spend this time and how their work is evaluated would be sought and acted upon.

In recent NEU polling,[119] 80% of teachers agreed with the statement that more professional teaching environments would lead to higher professional satisfaction levels and better teacher retention. They identified three essential criteria for being treated professionally:

- Involvement in workplace decision-making.
- Teacher opinion being taken seriously by the government and the public.
- A high degree of autonomy at work.

Teachers' perspectives are backed up by the OECD's Andreas Schleicher, who writes: 'In almost all TALIS countries/economies the extent to which teachers can participate in decision making has a strong positive association with the likelihood of reporting that teaching is a valued profession in society.'[120] The denial of these criteria leaves teachers feeling uninvolved, ignored and lacking autonomy in those areas of their work where they should be making professional choices.

A PROFESSIONAL APPROACH TO PEDAGOGY AND CURRICULUM

If teachers' voices are to be heard and their sense of themselves as professionals enhanced, the concept and practice of school leadership must be radically reformed. England's school leaders conceive their role to be one of monitoring teachers' performance. They spend, on their own admission, far less time working with teachers on pedagogical issues, including the curriculum and pupil assessment. This must change. If teaching is to be made more attractive as a profession, and if teachers are to find their work rewarding, the culture of fear and compliance that has taken root in too many schools must be eradicated.

Of course, leaders and managers must tackle poor performance: that is absolutely necessary if children and young people are not to be let down by a teacher who, for whatever reason, is unable to teach effectively. But monitoring in England's schools has become overbearing and, in many cases, has destroyed the professional respect that should be given to teachers who do the most complex work in education. The complexity, challenge and reach of teachers' work is well captured by Raewyn Connell, an Australian researcher who writes about the 'vital, elusive and fantastically complex' work that teachers do:

'Teaching involves connections: it consists of human encounters. These may be intense or formal, short or sustained, one-to-one or one-to-many … Encounter means interaction. Close-focus observation of classrooms shows this dramatically: the classroom is a busy place with lots going on at any given time. Pure top-down instruction is part, but only a minimal part, of actual teaching.

To play an effective role in some else's learning, any teacher must learn what that pupil's current capacities and motivations are, and what the pupil needs to take the next step in learning, the step after that, and so on. The teacher's capacity to learn about the pupils is a crucial element in teaching, perhaps the most important element in effective teaching. The more diverse the cohort, the greater is the professional demand upon the teacher to sustain the pupils' learning.

Classroom work includes complex intellectual labour: understanding the pupils and transforming the curriculum into classroom practice. This is an easily recognised part of the job. But the job also requires … what has come to be called emotional labour. This means creating connection with class members through encouragement, humour and sometimes anger; keeping focus in the classroom by managing pupils' boredom, excitement or distraction; dealing with conflict in the class and the effects of tension and trauma in the pupils' lives.'[121]

This passage captures the complexity and challenge of teachers' working days. It shows that any attempt to impose 'order' on teachers' work through rigid centralised lesson plans or 'scripts' that require teachers to conform to rigid stages in the lesson (such as standardised introductions and plenaries, and staged whole-class and small-group instruction) entirely misses the point of the enterprise. Teaching practice must be rooted in teachers' understanding of their classes, their understanding of the topic and their professional discretion to employ the teaching and learning strategies that they know are most appropriate at that particular moment.

If we are to improve standards of education then teachers must be freed to make informed professional choices. They must be given far greater 'task discretion' in their work. Of course, teachers should expect to justify their pedagogical choices when asked, but unless there is a concern about their work, those conversations – whether in appraisal meetings or more informally – should be situated on the fertile ground of mutual professional respect. There should be a frank acknowledgement by school leadership teams that teachers have more knowledge of their pupils and more expertise in adapting their practice to meet learning needs than someone who is observing and/or monitoring their practice. Leaders should learn, also, that any monitoring can only achieve very limited outcomes, because the metrics will always be too crude to capture what has really happened in a lesson. That is why conversations between equals, with the express aim of understanding each other better, are so essential. These conversations – leaders with teachers; teachers with each other – can support the creation and sustaining of a rich professional life.

The OECD strongly advocates schools as collaborative learning institutions where professional discussion and joint work among teachers and leaders on pedagogical practice – curriculum and assessment development, for example – are embedded in teacher and leaders' practice. The OECD is concerned that school leaders do not have time to give enough attention to what it calls 'instructional leadership'. Data from TALIS reveals that professional learning through collaboration is declining. The OECD warns that this is dangerous, arguing that if schools are not 'intellectually stimulating' places to work then 'disillusionment may creep in. Combine that with stress and an administration-heavy work environment and suddenly teaching becomes far too unattractive to be counted among society's most respected professions'.[122] This is a parlous state of affairs that the evidence in this book demonstrates has taken firm hold in England.

Let me state now that I strongly believe the majority of school leaders are highly professional, well informed, appreciative of their teachers and willing to support them in any way they can to achieve the best outcomes for pupils. I believe school leaders would love to initiate and support curriculum development projects and collaborative professional development. It is not their fault that too many of them feel compelled to monitor teachers rather than work with them, exercising real instructional leadership through collaboration and a ready acknowledgement of teachers' professional expertise. The sad truth is that school leaders feel most acutely the weight of the current school accountability framework, because their head is on the metaphorical chopping block should their school be found wanting. This framework is complex. It consists of league tables of school 'performance' that over-determine how a school's 'quality' is judged by the schools' inspectorate, Ofsted.

OFSTED NEEDS RADICAL REFORM

It is hard to overstate the shadow that Ofsted casts on our schools and on leaders and teachers. Chapter 3 details the extent to which the prospect of inspection adds to the pressures on teachers, as they struggle to provide 'evidence' for the inspectorate. It does not matter that Ofsted protests it does not need evidence, in the form of data and lesson planning, in particular formats, because while Ofsted can exercise its power to determine a school's quality in ways that are devoid of external scrutiny (who watches the watchmen?) then its power to dominate the school landscape will remain. School leaders, often misadvised by consultants, will latch on to what appears to have worked for other schools when they are inspected. And so the workload on teachers rises, even though so much of this work is useless.

The case against the validity and reliability of Ofsted judgements, and in particular their bias against schools in disadvantaged areas, is made in chapter 4. Here, in the concluding chapter, I want to propose a solution to the Ofsted issue.

I want to start by affirming that school accountability is necessary. Parents in particular have every right to know that their child is safe in school and that they are being taught well. Inadequate accountability leads to systemic injustices: the underachievement of Black students in the English education system for decades, to give just one example, and the current underachievement of Gypsy, Roma and Traveller children to give another.

But education professionals should be able to respect the inspectorate, which should be staffed by colleagues who are expert not only in the practice of teaching and learning, but also in the practice of inspection. They should be fully aware of the limitations of any inspection judgement. They should be cognisant that this is a snapshot of a school and that on other measures, in other weeks, with different subjects chosen for a 'deep dive', a different judgement could have been reached. Of course, Ofsted cannot admit this. In order to maintain its authority it can brook no questioning of the quality of its judgements – a stance that is increasingly untenable given the range and severity of the criticism it faces from informed sources.

It is clear that teachers deserve a better school inspectorate, one that is able to make valid and reliable judgements of school performance. In order to achieve this simple yet very demanding requirement, a new inspection agency is needed. Let's give it a name…

HER MAJESTY'S INSPECTORATE OF SCHOOLS

Her Majesty's Inspectorate of Schools would replace Ofsted and regional schools commissioners. Its remit would be to oversee the effective operation of the school accountability system to secure the best educational outcomes possible for children and young people.

Ofsted's network of additional inspectors would be replaced by a regional network of Her Majesty's Inspectors (HMIs). They would be accountable to the chief inspector, who would lead the inspectorate and produce an annual report on educational standards in England.

The chief inspector would lead teams of regional HMIs to develop a detailed knowledge of the challenges and opportunities facing schools in their region. The regional HMI team would have a range of professional experience and expertise across early years, primary, secondary and post-16 education, across subject areas, and with specialisms in SEND, equalities, leadership and so on. The HMIs would be experts in understanding and using data to bring about improvements in standards, and would use their specialist expertise to lead focused and targeted school inspections.

Schools would be supported by regional networks of advisers – expert education professionals who would work with schools to address specific challenges to improvement and/or weaknesses in their provision. Challenge advisers would follow the successful practice of the London Challenge and broker school-to-school support, enabling teachers and leaders to assist and learn from one another. Challenge advisers would also support schools facing recruitment and retention problems that adversely affect the standard of education they provide.

Each school would be responsible for using a national framework for school self-evaluation to examine its teaching, learning and assessment practices. This examination would lead to the production of a school development plan: a rigorous process that would identify areas of strength and weakness, and how weaknesses could be addressed in order to provide a consistently good standard of education. Schools with uneven provision would benefit from the support of the challenge advisers – subject and/or age-phase specialists who would work with school leaders and teachers to identify the most effective and productive improvement strategies and implement these successfully.

Schools would work in clusters, within the region, to participate in supportive and challenging peer review. These school clusters would facilitate school-to-school cooperation based on the sharing of best practice, in order to support one another to develop and improve. They would support pupils through managed moves and behaviour partnerships, and share resources where these could be better managed on a wider basis. School clusters would be able to draw on the support and advice of the challenge advisers in order to secure improvement across the cluster.

In addition to self-evaluation, schools would be benchmarked according to key indicators against other schools with comparable pupil intakes. Data would always be viewed in the round, alongside other evidence gained from the school's self-evaluation.

Regional HMI teams would use data, a school self-evaluation plan using the national framework for evaluation and, where necessary, targeted inspection focused on identified and sustained areas of a school's provision – for example, poor standards in a subject area, weaknesses in age-phase or in SEND provision, or weaknesses in leadership. Targeted and focused inspection would enable regional HMIs to use their finite resources wisely – something Ofsted has been unable to do.

HMI reports would give parents and governors, and other stakeholders, clear information about what has gone wrong and what needs to be done to secure improvement, as well as a timescale for achieving this before a follow-up inspection. Challenge advisers would work intensively in these schools to ensure they receive the regional support and help needed to secure a good standard of provision.

Parents would be able to report any concerns about their child's education to the regional HMI office. These concerns would be appropriately investigated and action instigated if it were judged necessary. Parents would be informed of what was being done to address their concerns. If regional HMIs had evidence that schools were not safe places, or were engaging in off-rolling or illegal exclusions, they would arrange for an inspection to ascertain the facts in each case and take swift action, if necessary, to stop schools behaving immorally and illegally.

Her Majesty's Inspectorate of Schools would employ a national team of specialist HMIs who would work with regional HMI teams to produce national survey reports on the strengths and weaknesses of education provision in their specialist area, drawing on the wealth of evidence in regional HMI teams. These reports would be used by schools and regional subject/age-phase advisers in order to share good practice and improve areas of weakness nationally in education.

The chief inspector would be responsible for the quality of judgements of regional HMI teams, ensuring that their judgements were valid, reliable and consistent across the regions. The inspectorate's findings and evidence of its approach to quality control would be publicly available and presented on a regular basis to Parliament.

This is just one of several recent proposals for Ofsted reform[123] and I present it in a spirit of debate and enquiry. I believe an intelligent inspection system would have expertise in the subject/age phase it was inspecting, would be proportionate to the scale of the problem, would be available when needed, and would gather data and information to generate and share good practice. An intelligent inspection system would be available to parents who, if their children are being educated in an academy, have virtually no resource beyond the school, other than contacting the education secretary via a website, to have their concerns addressed. This has led to huge scandals, particularly when parents have been alerted to and protested against the misuse of money by multi-academy trust CEOs, some of whom have leached the funding provided by the taxpayer away from their children's education and into companies run by the same CEO to provide inadequate and overpriced 'services' to the schools they control.

There are some signs that Ofsted is, finally, in the sights of the politicians.[124] The time for radical reform is approaching. Done properly, this will be one of the most important levers the government has to revive a confident, informed, collaborative teaching profession. It is overdue.

GOVERNMENT MUST DO LESS, BETTER

The encroaching reach of the long arm of national government into education policy and practice is documented in chapter 5. The acute problems of overactive but underprepared and badly managed government intervention – in curriculum, assessment and during the Covid-19 crisis – are evidence that government ministers and their Department for Education should do less and do that better.

The dislocation between the government, the civil service and educational professionals is evidenced in the startling finding that 82% of teachers believe the DfE has a negative impact on teaching and learning, while 74% think it is run incompetently.[125] This does not indicate a healthy relationship between the government and the profession – a relationship that deteriorated to even worse levels of distrust during the pandemic.

It is not as though the government does not have a proper and key role in determining education policy. Through expert use of the best available evidence, both national and international, the OECD advises governments to:

- Prioritise the activities that have the greatest impact on teachers' practices.
- Include teachers in decision-making at school.
- Strengthen peer collaboration.
- Build collaborative school cultures.
- Strengthen the links between teacher appraisal and CPD.
- Link professional autonomy with a collaborative culture.
- Involve teachers in developing professional standards.
- Strengthen teacher leadership.
- Engage teachers in educational reform.
- Build teachers' capacity to use technology innovatively and effectively in the classroom.[126]

Looking at this list, I am struck by how little correlation there is between the OECD's recommendations and government interventions in education in the past decade. What the OECD points to is a concerted and sustained effort to build a strong, informed and resilient teaching profession with a real stake in the quality standards by which it is held accountable. The OECD focus is on collaboration, a professional stake in standards, and a voice for the profession in education policy and reform.

In England, instead, we have experienced government policy intervention that has not involved the profession. DfE consultations are renowned for the skewing of consultation questions towards a predetermined outcome, relying too heavily on a tight cadre of trusted educationalists whose views closely align with the government's thinking. The DfE has had a simplistic view of policy implementation, believing that its job has ended when regulations or guidance are sent out to schools. It has failed to understand the complexities of implementing policy in a fragmented school system where, frankly, DfE documents proliferate unread on the school leader's desk, whereas Ofsted missives are scrutinised minutely for their implications and are too often taken as a call to action that loads more work on to teachers' already over-burdened shoulders.

The result has been a miasma of unintended outcomes. Despite the best ministerial intentions, teachers have clearly not been liberated from excessive government intervention or from mountains of bureaucracy. They have certainly not been awarded their promised 'freedom'. The opposite is true and the consequences for the profession in terms of its appalling retention rates – and for the nation's children and young people in terms of the widening attainment gap between poor children and their more advantaged peers – are clear and, for the government, highly inconvenient. No amount of talk about 'levelling up' will change the data that shows educational outcomes are becoming more unequal after more than a decade of frenetic reform intended to achieve the opposite.

The truth is that the extent of existing government policy makes it incomprehensible. To give just one example, in 2019 the government launched a new archive of guidance for school governors. For stakeholders in both academy and maintained schools, it was intended as a reference tool to ensure that duties under government legislation were fully accessible and fully understood. The archive contains guidance on: SRE policy; safeguarding; SEND; teaching and learning; offsite activities and trips; complaints policy; behaviour policy; accessibility policy; attendance and punctuality policy; anti-bullying policy; EAL policy; evaluating and developing teaching and learning; literacy policy; and numeracy policy. More than 2,494 web pages and A4 pages of advice were issued for maintained schools and more than 1,971 for academies. As the researchers who uncovered this 'black hole' of published materials note, 'for a school governor in a voluntary, part-time role, [this] is obviously overwhelming, and much of this guidance must inevitably remain unread'.[127]

It is simply wrong that government ministers have such unfettered power over the national curriculum and its assessment. While this power has been convenient, allowing ministers to drive through radical changes to the national curriculum, national assessment arrangements and qualification reform, it is not sustainable to make successful education policy in this way. We see the consequences now: in the informed and influential voices declaring that the national curriculum ignores the development of the skills base that employers need from school leavers; in the protests of marginalised groups who see their contribution to knowledge excised from the taught curriculum; and in the information provided by education policy think tanks that are exposing the narrowness of the subject base at A level, clearly an unintended outcome of the 2014 reforms to GCSE and A level.[128]

So, alongside my proposal for a new inspection agency, I present a modest proposal to create an independent body to limit direct ministerial intervention in core education matters. Chapter 5 has shown the extent of the chaos and confusion generated when politicians drive through rapid change to the curriculum and national assessment that is highly contested and ignores stakeholder views. As the uncertain and inadequate capabilities of recent office-holders have clearly demonstrated, curriculum and assessment reform is simply too important to be left to whoever holds office as education secretary and schools minister. Reform of these core educational practices should be cyclical, well planned and carefully implemented, with full involvement from a range of stakeholders, including the government, the profession, researchers and academics, employers and parents. To accomplish this, a new body would be created...

THE NATIONAL EDUCATION ENTITLEMENT COUNCIL

This body would have a remit to:

- Oversee the introduction of the national curriculum as an entitlement for all children and young people in all state-funded schools.
- Oversee the development of a qualifications framework to raise standards of achievement nationally.

Both the curriculum and the qualifications framework and content would be founded on these principles:

- Be age-appropriate and broad and balanced, ensuring entitlement for all pupils to the arts and humanities.
- Contain a range of subjects including academic, social, vocational and technical education.
- Embed equality, diversity and inclusion in all subject areas.

- Be slim and flexible enough to include local curriculum entitlements and to enable schools to adapt it according to their local circumstances, recognising and working towards equity in access, experience and outcomes.
- Offer flexibility and meaningful choice of subjects and ways of learning for all, and be accessible to, inclusive of and engaging for all learners, including those with SEND and EAL.
- Be culturally inclusive.
- Be linked to a qualifications system based on a unified framework that enables student progress and links to lifelong learning.

Crucially, the National Education Entitlement Council would direct curriculum and assessment reform that could be well managed by teachers on a rolling timescale, taking different subjects at different times on a cyclical basis. This would enable teachers to engage with the consultation process. It would give them time to consider how best to embed the changes to the curriculum and its assessment into their teaching, including proper consideration of the range of their pupils' abilities and those with SEND. Teaching strategies could be developed collaboratively.

Such an approach would not only engage the profession and other stakeholders, but also create space for informed and rational discussion on issues that would benefit greatly from an evidence-based approach. For example, whether GCSEs at 16 should be retained when young people remain in education until they are 18. Is there a need for such a high-stakes hurdle at this stage? What can be done about the 'forgotten third' who fail to reach a grade 4 at GCSE and find their path to further education or an apprenticeship blocked? Surely these issues deserve serious debate – debate that, at present, is over-heightened by entrenched positions.

Changes to the curriculum and its assessment go to the heart of teachers' practice. The profession has the right to be consulted on them and for them to be well planned with adequate lead-in times for implementation. Taking these changes out of direct government intervention and away from a DfE that has inadequate capacity to do them well seems to me a no-brainer.

AND FINALLY – TO TEACHERS THEMSELVES

I have worked in education as a teacher, a member of a school leadership team, a lecturer training teachers, a head of education in a university and as the general secretary and joint general secretary of two unions. During those 40 years in education, I have witnessed the erosion of teacher authority and autonomy – and the consequences of that erosion on teachers' desire and willingness to remain in their chosen profession.

There is no doubt in my mind – and I think the evidence of this book shows – that teachers need to regain proper autonomy and authority within their schools and with government. They deserve better. One aim in writing this book is to bear witness to the work teachers do and, through an evidence-based approach drawing on international comparisons, to show that it does not have to be this way. I have put forward compelling evidence of the unsustainable and, frankly, often ludicrous demands made of teachers and the squandering of their time. High education standards cannot be built on the back of an exhausted and demoralised profession. Given other options, too many teachers leave the profession too early. Their developing expertise and experience are lost to their schools and to the pupils they taught.

The crisis in teacher supply will continue until the government and its agencies understand and acknowledge the complexity and skill of the work that teachers do; until they develop and effectively implement policies that support teachers to do good work; until pointless, exhausting work is eliminated from teachers' working lives; and until there is radical reform of the accountability system, including Ofsted, which drives so much of this work. Children and young people will continue to be let down because there are not enough teachers qualified in the right subjects to teach them.

To teachers I say this. Join a union and work with your colleagues in school to reclaim your voice and reassert your expertise and experience. Work with your teaching colleagues to confidently claim your individual and collective right to be consulted on professional issues such as approaches to teaching and learning and assessment. Any school leader who really believes in distributed leadership will welcome these discussions, seriously engage in them and work with their teaching colleagues to achieve consensual change in their school.

Covid-19 showed parents and the public just how demanding and vital is the work that teachers do. Now is the time to build on that recognition, that new-found respect for the profession, and to start to turn the tide on excessive, intensive and unnecessary work that leaves teachers too little time for their families, for their hobbies, even to live healthy lives. Now is the time to assert that mental ill health and physical exhaustion are not the necessary evils of being a teacher.

Now is the time for teachers to realise that they are in short supply. They are a precious commodity whose resources must be well used and whose expertise must be properly understood and respected by school leaders, by policymakers, by the inspectorate and by government.

Now is the time for change – for teaching to become, once again, a profession that young people can commit to for the long haul. This would be the single biggest factor in raising standards of education, most particularly for poor children and young people, who most need the best and most experienced teachers.

ACKNOWLEDGEMENTS

I could not have written this book without the support of many colleagues and friends. In particular I want to thank my NEU colleagues, who were so generous with their time when I wandered into their offices and asked 'Do you have a moment?' to talk through the ideas I was wrestling with. Andrew Baisley, recently named 'Geek of the Week' on ITV's *Peston* show, provided the data analysis of Ofsted judgements mapped against pupil intakes, and checked my understanding of the TALIS data and of school funding trends. David Powell assiduously kept me right on teacher supply, pay trends and data. Robin Bevan directed me to research on effective school-led CPD. And Kevin Courtney, my co joint general secretary, was unfailingly supportive and one of the first readers of the draft manuscript.

Martin Johnson, my husband, read chapter drafts as they were written and took on the onerous and thankless task of checking references. My editor, Isla McMillan, was meticulous in her checking of facts and references, and suggested chapter headings and subtitles that were just right. But my greatest thanks are to Donna Buttle, my personal assistant. It was she who kept me in order: saving the numerous versions of each chapter, making them look respectable, and inserting graphs and data where required.

To everyone who encouraged me to 'keep going' – thank you. And now I might be able to think, and talk, about something else!

ENDNOTES

1   Department for Education. (2020) 'Academic year 2020/21: initial teacher training census', https://explore-education-statistics.service.gov.uk/find-statistics/initial-teacher-training-census/2020-21

2   Martin, M. (2022) 'ITT applications plummet 24%', TES, www.tes.com/magazine/news/general/itt-teacher-training-recruitment-applications-plummet-24

3   OECD. (2019) *TALIS 2018 Results (Volume I): teachers and school leaders as lifelong learners*, table 1.4.2, https://doi.org/10.1787/1d0bc92a-en

4   TUC. (2019) 'Workers in the UK put in more than £32 billion worth of unpaid overtime last year – TUC analysis', www.tuc.org.uk/news/workers-uk-put-more-ps32-billion-worth-unpaid-overtime-last-year-tuc-analysis

5   Jerrim, J, & Sims, S. (2019) *The Teaching and Learning International Survey (TALIS) 2018: research report*, UCL, Institute of Education, page 82, table 3.2.1, https://dera.ioe.ac.uk//33612/1/TALIS_2018_research.pdf

6   OECD. (2020) *TALIS 2018 Results (Volume II): teachers and school leaders as valued professionals*, figure 11.2.9, https://doi.org/10.1787/19cf08df-en (England's data extrapolated against OECD average for sources of teacher stress)

7   Allen, B, & McInerney, L. (2019) *The Recruitment Gap: attracting teachers to schools serving disadvantaged communities*, The Sutton Trust, www.suttontrust.com/wp-content/uploads/2019/12/The-Recruitment-Gap.pdf

8   Department for Education. (2021) 'School workforce in England: teacher retention', https://explore-education-statistics.service.gov.uk/find-statistics/school-workforce-in-england

9   Department for Education. (2021) 'School workforce in England: entrants, leavers and changes in working pattern', https://explore-education-statistics.service.gov.uk/find-statistics/school-workforce-in-england

10   Department for Education. (2021) 'School workforce in England: teacher retention', https://explore-education-statistics.service.gov.uk/find-statistics/school-workforce-in-england

11   School Teachers' Review Body. (2021) *School Teachers' Review Body 31st Report 2021*, page 46, figure 8, https://assets.publishing.service.gov.uk/government/uploads/system/uploads/attachment_data/file/1005678/STRB_2021_Web_Accessible.pdf

12   Department for Education. (2017) *Analysis of School and Teacher Level Factors Relating to Teacher Supply*, https://assets.publishing.service.gov.uk/government/uploads/system/uploads/attachment_data/file/682023/SFR86_2017_Main_Text.pdf

13   Department for Education, the Rt Hon Nick Clegg and the Rt Hon Baroness Nicky Morgan. (2015) 'Government pledges to reduce teacher workload' (press release), www.gov.uk/government/news/government-pledges-to-reduce-teacher-workload

14   Jerrim, J, & Sims, S. (2019) *The Teaching and Learning International Survey (TALIS) 2018: research report*, UCL, Institute of Education, https://dera.ioe.ac.uk//33612/1/TALIS_2018_research.pdf

15   Walker, M, Worth, J, & Van den Brande, J. (National Foundation for Educational Research). (2019) *Teacher Workload Survey 2019: research report*, Department for Education, https://assets.publishing.service.gov.uk/government/uploads/system/uploads/attachment_data/file/855933/teacher_workload_survey_2019_main_report_amended.pdf

16   National Audit Office. (2017) *Retaining and Developing the Teaching Workforce*, www.nao.org.uk/wp-content/uploads/2017/09/Retaining-and-developing-the-teaching-workforce.pdf

17   Department for Education. (2019) *Teacher Recruitment and Retention Strategy*, https://assets.publishing.service.gov.uk/government/uploads/system/uploads/attachment_data/file/786856/DFE_Teacher_Retention_Strategy_Report.pdf

18   Ibid., page 8

19   OECD. (2020) *TALIS 2018 Results (Volume II): teachers and school leaders as valued professionals*, figure 11.2.10, https://doi.org/10.1787/19cf08df-en

20   Nick Gibb was schools minister from 2010 to 2012. He was sacked in a reshuffle in September 2012, but returned to the DfE as school reform minister in July 2014 and served again as schools minister from 2015 to 2021. He was sacked by Boris Johnson in the September 2021 reshuffle, having outlasted five education secretaries.

21   Department for Education. (2021) *Initial Teacher Training (ITT) Market Review Report*, https://assets.publishing.service.gov.uk/government/uploads/system/uploads/attachment_data/file/999621/ITT_market_review_report.pdf

22   Schwabe, M. (2019) *Country Note: England (UK) – results from TALIS 2018*, OECD, page 3, www.oecd.org/education/talis/TALIS2018_CN_ENG.pdf

23   NEU analysis reveals that 61% of teachers in English state primary schools in the top quintile of pupils receiving free school meals (FSM) are aged under 40,

compared with 52% in the lowest quintile. In English state secondary schools, 61% of teachers in the most deprived schools measured on FSM are aged under 40, compared with 49% in the least deprived schools.

24   Walker, M, Straw, S, Worth, J, & Grayson, H. (National Foundation for Educational Research). (2018) *Early Career CPD: exploratory research – research report*, Department for Education, https://assets.publishing.service.gov.uk/government/uploads/system/uploads/attachment_data/file/916492/Early_career_CPD-exploratory_research.pdf

25   Department for Education. (2019) *Early Career Framework*, https://assets.publishing.service.gov.uk/government/uploads/system/uploads/attachment_data/file/978358/Early-Career_Framework_April_2021.pdf

26   TES. (2021) 'Third of heads fear new teachers will quit over ECF', www.tes.com/magazine/news/general/third-heads-fear-new-teachers-will-quit-over-ecf

27   Jerrim, J, & Sims, S. (2019) *The Teaching and Learning International Survey (TALIS) 2018: research report*, UCL, Institute of Education, page 19, https://dera.ioe.ac.uk//33612/1/TALIS_2018_research.pdf

28   Fletcher-Wood, H, & Zuccollo, J. (2020) *The Effects of High-Quality Professional Development on Teachers and Students: a rapid review and meta-analysis*, Education Policy Institute, https://epi.org.uk/wp-content/uploads/2020/02/EPI-Wellcome_CPD-Review__2020.pdf

29   OECD. (2019) *TALIS 2018 Results (Volume I): teachers and school leaders as lifelong learners*, page 158, https://doi.org/10.1787/1d0bc92a-en

30   Grissom, JA. (2011) 'Can good principals keep teachers in disadvantaged schools? Linking principal effectiveness to teacher satisfaction and turnover in hard-to-staff environments', *Teachers College Record*, 113(11), 2552-2585

31   Kraft, MA, & Papay, JP. (2014) 'Can professional environments in schools promote teacher development? Explaining heterogeneity in returns to teaching experience', *Educational Evaluation and Policy Analysis*, 36(4), 476-500

32   OECD. (2019) *TALIS 2018 Results (Volume I): teachers and school leaders as lifelong learners*, https://doi.org/10.1787/1d0bc92a-en
OECD. (2020) *TALIS 2018 Results (Volume II): teachers and school leaders as valued professionals*, https://doi.org/10.1787/19cf08df-en

33   OECD. (2020) *TALIS 2018 Results (Volume II): teachers and school leaders as valued professionals*, figure 11.4.9, https://doi.org/10.1787/19cf08df-en

34   Ibid., figure 11.4.11

35   Ibid., figure 11.4.12

36   Ibid., figure 11.4.8

37   Ibid., figure 11.5.9

38   Ibid., page 148

39   Schleicher, A. (2015) *Schools for 21st-Century Learners: strong leaders,
      confident teachers, innovative approaches*, OECD, page 55, http://dx.doi.
      org/10.1787/9789264231191-en

40   OECD. (2020) *TALIS 2018 Results (Volume II): teachers and school leaders as
      valued professionals*, figure 11.5.4, https://doi.org/10.1787/19cf08df-en

41   Ibid., figure 11.2.8

42   Green, F. (2021) 'British teachers' declining job quality: evidence from the Skills and
      Employment Survey', *Oxford Review of Education*, 47(3), 386-403

43   Ibid.

44   Andreas Schleicher speaking at the launch of the 2021 edition of the OECD's
      annual *Education at a Glance* report on 16 September 2021.

45   All references to NEU teacher and leader members in this chapter are taken from a
      Delta poll of 1,746 NEU teacher and leader members conducted in May 2021. Data
      was weighted to be representative of all members by gender, age, region, school
      type and school sector. Data was correct to within +/- 2.3% at the 95% confidence
      interval.

46   Spielman, A. (2018) 'HMCI commentary: curriculum and the new education
      inspection framework', www.gov.uk/government/speeches/hmci-commentary-
      curriculum-and-the-new-education-inspection-framework

47   Bill and Melinda Gates Foundation, Measures of Effective Teaching project: https://
      usprogram.gatesfoundation.org/news-and-insights/articles/measures-of-effective-
      teaching-project

48   Richmond, T. (2019) *Requires Improvement: a new role for Ofsted and school
      inspections*, EDSK, www.edsk.org/wp-content/uploads/2019/04/Requires-
      Improvement.pdf

49   National Audit Office. (2018) *Ofsted's Inspection of Schools*, page 9, www.nao.org.
      uk/wp-content/uploads/2018/05/Ofsteds-inspection-of-schools.pdf

50   Richmond, T. (2019) 'Ofsted's worrying reliability findings won't comfort heads
      who get "the call" in a couple of months', *Schools Week*, https://schoolsweek.co.uk/
      ofsteds-worrying-reliability-findings-wont-comfort-heads-who-get-the-call-in-a-
      couple-of-months

51   Ibid.

52   Bousted, M. (2019) 'How will Ofsted achieve such lofty ambitions?', TES, www.tes.
      com/news/how-will-ofsted-achieve-such-lofty-ambitions

53   Gibson, S, Oliver, L, & Dennison, M. (2015) *Workload Challenge: Analysis of
      Teacher Consultation Responses – research report*, Department for Education,
      https://assets.publishing.service.gov.uk/government/uploads/system/uploads/
      attachment_data/file/401406/RR445_-_Workload_Challenge_-_Analysis_of_
      teacher_consultation_responses_FINAL.pdf

54 Hazell, W. (2021) 'Two-thirds of parents don't look at Ofsted inspection reports when choosing a school, poll finds', *iNews*, https://inews.co.uk/news/education/osfted-reports-inspection-ratings-parents-dont-care-choose-school-yougov-poll-1275609

55 Woolcock, N, & Papworth, H. (2021) 'Teachers condemn Ofsted "reign of terror"', *The Times*, www.thetimes.co.uk/article/teachers-condemn-ofsted-reign-of-terror-inspections-rwt5wkf9r

56 Churchill, H. (2018) 'Austerity adversely targets children in need' (blog post), Social Policy Association, www.social-policy.org.uk/50-for-50/austerity-children

57 TUC. (2019) 'Child poverty in working households up by 800,000 since 2010, says TUC', www.tuc.org.uk/news/child-poverty-working-households-800000-2010-says-tuc

58 Child Poverty Action Group. 'Child poverty facts and figures', updated March 2021. https://cpag.org.uk/child-poverty/child-poverty-facts-and-figures

59 Staton, B. (2021) 'UK Budget fails to deliver "skills revolution", say education leaders', *Financial Times*, www.ft.com/content/b0199edc-d7f7-4d75-b23c-4fd78cb5ee75

60 Institute for Fiscal Studies. (2021) 'Education spending – further education and sixth forms', https://ifs.org.uk/education-spending/Further-Education-and-Sixth-Forms

61 Sibieta, L. (2020) 'Larger funding cuts for schools in poor areas leave them badly placed to deal with COVID-19 challenges' (press release), Institute for Fiscal Studies, https://ifs.org.uk/publications/15026

62 Sibieta, L. (2021) *School Spending in England: trends over time and future outlook*, Institute for Fiscal Studies, https://ifs.org.uk/uploads/BN334-School-spending-in-England-trends-over-time-and-future-outlook.pdf

63 Hall, R, & Adams, R. (2021) 'Per pupil spending in English schools to fall to under 2009-10 levels – IFS', *The Guardian*, www.theguardian.com/education/2021/sep/02/per-pupil-spending-in-english-schools-to-fall-to-under-2009-10-levels-ifs

64 Andrews, J, Hutchinson, J, & Johnes, R. (2016) *Grammar Schools and Social Mobility*, Education Policy Institute, page 6, https://epi.org.uk/publications-and-research/grammar-schools-social-mobility

65 Gregory, A. (2021) 'Thousands of adverse birth outcomes in England down to "alarming" inequality', *The Guardian*, www.theguardian.com/lifeandstyle/2021/nov/01/thousands-of-adverse-birth-outcomes-in-england-down-to-alarming-inequality

66 Hall, R, & Adams, R. (2021) 'Per pupil spending in English schools to fall to under 2009-10 levels – IFS', *The Guardian*, www.theguardian.com/education/2021/sep/02/per-pupil-spending-in-english-schools-to-fall-to-under-2009-10-levels-ifs

67 National Audit Office. (2018) *Financial Sustainability of Local Authorities 2018*, www.nao.org.uk/wp-content/uploads/2018/03/Financial-sustainabilty-of-local-authorites-2018.pdf

68   Smith, G, Sylva, K, Smith, T, Sammons, P, & Omonigho, A. (2018) *Stop Start: Survival, Decline or Closure? Children's centres in England, 2018*, The Sutton Trust, www.suttontrust.com/wp-content/uploads/2018/04/StopStart-FINAL.pdf

69   Churchill, H. (2018) 'Austerity adversely targets children in need' (blog post), Social Policy Association, www.social-policy.org.uk/50-for-50/austerity-children

70   Booth, R. (2021) 'Twice as many youth services in England's richest areas – survey', *The Guardian*, www.theguardian.com/society/2021/nov/01/twice-as-many-youth-services-in-englands-richest-areas-survey

71   Churchill, H. (2018) 'Austerity adversely targets children in need' (blog post), Social Policy Association, www.social-policy.org.uk/50-for-50/austerity-children

72   Mason, R, & Allegretti, A. (2021) 'Gavin Williamson should be sacked over exam failures, says Keir Starmer', *The Guardian*, www.theguardian.com/politics/2021/aug/11/keir-starmer-gavin-williamson-sacked-pandemic-failures

73   Data analysed from Ofsted's Get Information About Schools service: https://get-information-schools.service.gov.uk/Downloads

74   Carr, J. (2021) 'Spielman says deprived schools' lower grades offset by leadership praise', *Schools Week*, https://schoolsweek.co.uk/spielman-says-deprived-schools-lower-grades-offset-by-leadership-praise

75   Hazell, W. (2021) 'Two-thirds of parents don't look at Ofsted inspection reports when choosing a school, poll finds', *iNews*, https://inews.co.uk/news/education/osfted-reports-inspection-ratings-parents-dont-care-choose-school-yougov-poll-1275609

76   National Audit Office. (2018) *Ofsted's Inspection of Schools*, page 9, www.nao.org.uk/wp-content/uploads/2018/05/Ofsteds-inspection-of-schools.pdf

77   Hutchinson, J. (2016) *School Inspection in England: is there room to improve?*, Education Policy Institute, https://epi.org.uk/wp-content/uploads/2018/01/school-inspection-in-england-web.pdf

78   Allen, B, & McInerney, L. (2019) *The Recruitment Gap: attracting teachers to schools serving disadvantaged communities*, The Sutton Trust, www.suttontrust.com/wp-content/uploads/2019/12/The-Recruitment-Gap.pdf

79   Timmins, N. (2021) *Schools and Coronavirus: the government's handling of education during the pandemic*, Institute for Government, page 4, www.instituteforgovernment.org.uk/sites/default/files/publications/schools-and-coronavirus.pdf

80   Gove, M. (2013) 'The progressive betrayal', speech to the Social Market Foundation, www.smf.co.uk/michael-gove-speaks-at-the-smf

81   Hutchinson, J. Reader, M, & Akhal, A. (2020) *Education in England: annual report 2020*, Education Policy Institute, https://epi.org.uk/wp-content/uploads/2020/09/EPI_2020_Annual_Report_.pdf

82   Ibid., page 18

83   This data is drawn from the Department for Education's performance data. We have compared the percentage of pupils in 2016 achieving five or more A*-C GCSEs or equivalents, including A*-C in English and maths, with the percentage of pupils in 2019 achieving strong 9-5 passes in English and maths GCSEs.

84   www.ibe.unesco.org/en/glossary-curriculum-terminology/i/inclusive-curriculum

85   Rudolph, S, Sriprakash, A, & Gerrard, J. (2018) 'Knowledge and racial violence: the shine and shadow of "powerful knowledge"', *Ethics and Education*, 13(1), 22-38

86   Williams, R. (1958) *Culture and Society*, Hogarth Press, page 187

87   Ferguson, D. (2021) 'Home schooling: "I'm a maths lecturer – and I had to get my children to teach me"', The Guardian, www.theguardian.com/education/2021/feb/20/im-a-maths-lecturer-and-i-had-to-get-my-children-to-teach-me

88   Kellaway, L. (2021) 'What is the point of schools?', *Financial Times*, www.ft.com/content/13231302-8443-4652-b751-4082a936b282

89   Andreas Schleicher delivering a presentation titled 'Key findings from TALIS 2018' at an Education Policy Institute event on 19 June 2019.

90   Ferguson, D. (2021) 'Home schooling: "I'm a maths lecturer – and I had to get my children to teach me"', *The Guardian*, www.theguardian.com/education/2021/feb/20/im-a-maths-lecturer-and-i-had-to-get-my-children-to-teach-me

91   CBI. (2019) 'Education system leaving young people unprepared for the modern world', www.cbi.org.uk/media-centre/articles/education-system-leaving-young-people-unprepared-for-modern-world

92   Schleicher, A. (2018) *Valuing Our Teachers and Raising Their Status: how communities can help*, OECD Publishing, page 14, www.oecd.org/education/valuing-our-teachers-and-raising-their-status-9789264292697-en.htm

93   Ibid., page 9

94   White, J. (2018) 'The weakness of "powerful knowledge"', *London Review of Education*, 16(2), 325-335

95   Wall, P, Warriner, J, & Luck, B. (2021) *The Need For Stability: extract – presenting problems*, Edpol.net, www.edpol.net/wp-content/uploads/2021/05/20200528-Need-for-education-policy-stability-27.4.21-v-4.2-presenting-problems.pdf

96   Department for Education. (2010) *The Importance of Teaching: the schools white paper 2010*, https://assets.publishing.service.gov.uk/government/uploads/system/uploads/attachment_data/file/175429/CM-7980.pdf

97   Arnold, M. (1869) *Culture and Anarchy: an essay in political and social criticism*

98   Pollard, A. (2012) 'Proposed primary curriculum: what about the pupils?', IOE London Blog, https://ioelondonblog.wordpress.com/2012/06/12/.proposed-primary-curriculum-what-about-the-pupils

99   Gove, M. (2013) 'I refuse to surrender to the Marxist teachers hell-bent on destroying our schools: Education Secretary berates "the new enemies of promise" for opposing his plans', *The Daily Mail*, www.dailymail.co.uk/debate/article-

2298146/I-refuse-surrender-Marxist-teachers-hell-bent-destroying-schools-Education-Secretary-berates-new-enemies-promise-opposing-plans.html

100   Bousted, M. (2016) 'Like a horror show: It is difficult to comprehend the government's stupidity over testing in schools', TES, www.tes.com/magazine/archive/horror-show-it-difficult-comprehend-governments-stupidity-over-testing-schools

101   Neumann, E, Towers, E, Gewirtz, S, & Maguire, M. (2016) *A Curriculum For All? The effects of recent key stage 4 curriculum, assessment and accountability reforms on English secondary education*, King's College London, http://downloads2.dodsmonitoring.com/downloads/Misc_Files/KingsCollege141116.pdf

102   OECD. (2020) *TALIS 2018 Results (Volume II): teachers and school leaders as valued professionals*, figure 11.5.12, https://doi.org/10.1787/19cf08df-en

103   Department for Education. (2017) *Analysis of School and Teacher Level Factors Relating to Teacher Supply*, https://assets.publishing.service.gov.uk/government/uploads/system/uploads/attachment_data/file/682023/SFR86_2017_Main_Text.pdf

104   Timmins, N. (2021) *Schools and Coronavirus: the government's handling of education during the pandemic*, Institute for Government, page 7, www.instituteforgovernment.org.uk/sites/default/files/publications/schools-and-coronavirus.pdf

105   Ibid.

106   Ibid., page 16

107   Data from a 2021 Deltapoll of NEU members

108   *Macbeth*, Act 5, scene 5, lines 26-28

109   Achtaridou, E, Mason, E, Behailu, A, Steill, B, Willis, B, & Coldwell, M. (2022) *School Recovery Strategies: year 1 findings – research report*, Department for Education/Government Social Research, https://assets.publishing.service.gov.uk/government/uploads/system/uploads/attachment_data/file/1045471/School_Recovery_Strategies_year_1_findings.pdf

110   Ibid., page 34

111   Ibid., page 35

112   Ibid., page 35

113   Cribb, J, & Sibieta, L. (2021) 'The long, long squeeze on teacher pay', Institute for Fiscal Studies, https://ifs.org.uk/publications/15552

114   Ibid.

115   School Teachers' Review Body. (2018) *School Teachers' Review Body: 28th report*, page 41, https://assets.publishing.service.gov.uk/government/uploads/system/uploads/attachment_data/file/728381/CCS207_CCS0518679568-1_STRB_Book_Web_accessible.pdf

116   National Audit Office. (2017) *Retaining and Developing the School Workforce*, page 8, www.nao.org.uk/wp-content/uploads/2017/09/Retaining-and-developing-the-teaching-workforce.pdf

117   Department for Education. (2021) *Government Evidence to the STRB: the 2021 pay award*, page 7, https://assets.publishing.service.gov.uk/government/uploads/system/uploads/attachment_data/file/967761/STRB_Written_Evidence_2021.pdf

118   Department for Education. (Updated 2021) 'Guidance: flexible working in schools', www.gov.uk/government/publications/flexible-working-in-schools/flexible-working-in-schools--2

119   NEU Deltapoll fieldwork, 19-26 May 2021. Base: NEU members in England and Wales

120   Schleicher, A. (2016) *Teaching Excellence Through Professional Learning and Policy Reform: lessons from around the world*, OECD Publishing, page 48, http://dx.doi.org/10.1787/9789264252059-en

121   Connell, R. (2021) 'Vital, elusive and fantastically complex: teacher's worth', *Journal of Professional Learning*, https://cpl.asn.au/journal/semester-2-2021/vital-elusive-and-fantastically-complex-teacher-s-worth

122   OECD. (2020) *TALIS 2018 Results (Volume II): teachers and school leaders as valued professionals*, https://doi.org/10.1787/19cf08df-en

123   See also:
Richmond, T. (2019) *Requires Improvement: a new role for Ofsted and school inspections*, EDSK, www.edsk.org/wp-content/uploads/2019/04/Requires-Improvement.pdf
Mansfield, I, & Clark, T. (2020) *The Watchmen Revisited: curriculum and faith in Ofsted's new inspection framework*, Policy Exchange, https://policyexchange.org.uk/wp-content/uploads/The-Watchmen-Revisited.pdf

124   Whittaker, F. (2021) 'Improver and inspector: Green fleshes out Ofsted reform proposals', *Schools Week*, https://schoolsweek.co.uk/improver-and-inspector-green-fleshes-out-ofsted-reform-proposals

125   2021 Deltapoll of NEU members

126   Schleicher, A. (2016) *Teaching Excellence Through Professional Learning and Policy Reform: lessons from around the world*, OECD Publishing, chapter 3, http://dx.doi.org/10.1787/9789264252059-en

127   Wall, P, Warriner, J, & Luck, B. (2021) *The Need For Stability: extract – presenting problems*, Edpol.net, www.edpol.net/wp-content/uploads/2021/05/20200528-Need-for-education-policy-stability-27.4.21-v-4.2-presenting-problems.pdf

128   Robinson, D, and Bunting, F. (2021) *A Narrowing Path to Success? 16-19 curriculum breath and employment outcomes*, Education Policy Institute/The Royal Society, https://epi.org.uk/wp-content/uploads/2021/09/EPI-Royal_Society-16-19-report.pdf